Learning disabilities, **sex** & the law

A PRACTICAL GUIDE

Claire Fanstone and Sarah Andrews

Foreword by Hilary Brown, Professor of Social Care
Canterbury Christ Church University College

D0993750

fpa

putting sexual health on
the agenda

Acknowledgements

The help we received while putting this publication together was invaluable. We would like to thank:

Julie Biggs
Karen Brewer
Professor Hilary Brown
Angie Brown-Simpson
Cate Dandridge
Caroline Davey
Pat Grey
Zarine Katrak
Stephen Lightley
Rob Macmillan
Margaret McGovern
Vivienne Quant
Angela Reynolds
Anne Robson
Terri Ryland
Scott Saunders
Jo Skitteral
Juliana Slobodian
Kathryn Stone
Anne Weyman OBE
Georgina Whitfield
Former and present staff of **fpa** in Wales

Special thanks are due to Richard Kramer from Turning Point for giving so much of his time and expertise, and helping us to clarify the legal information.

With thanks to Glynis Murphy and Tony Holland for their help with the 2nd edition.

Foreword

S*ex and the Law* reflects the law as it affects people with intellectual disabilities and those involved in their care. It sets out, in a clear question and answer format, the key principles, definitions and frameworks that should govern decision making in this complex arena.

As the authors make clear, the law does two things. It is framed to ensure that people with learning disabilities are both:

- enabled and supported to exercise the same rights as other citizens when it comes to their sexual choices *and*
- protected as citizens from sexual violence or exploitation.

These rights are enshrined in the ordinary criminal law, which has additional provisions which make it an offence to have sex with someone who cannot understand enough to consent or whose need for assistance means that they would be under too much pressure to refuse, for example at the hands of a family member or care worker.

Empowerment and protection are sometimes talked about as if they were mutually exclusive but this can lead to compromise rather than a clear commitment to do both well. All citizens are entitled both to a sexual life of our own choice, and to equal protection before the law if our rights or bodily integrity is violated. These are not alternatives – they are both vital to our personal fulfilment and safety. People with learning disabilities deserve this as do we all. If they are wronged, they have a right to access justice on an equitable basis and to be given whatever support they need in order to act as credible witnesses and seek appropriate redress. This book also addresses some of the issues affecting people with learning disabilities whose sexual behaviour may be inappropriate or upsetting.

This book will help to dispel myths which undermine this very clear commitment. It will enable you to work confidently and to use your 'common' sense, ensuring that the law does not hold you back but empowers you to act in the interests of people with learning disabilities who look to you, and to your service, for information, support and protection.

Hilary Brown
Professor of Social Care, Canterbury Christ Church University College

How to use this publication

The law in the book relates to England and Wales only. Law in Scotland and Northern Ireland differs to this.

The book is in three main sections.

Sex, the law and people with learning disabilities
The questions included in the publication are commonly asked questions which we have heard from many staff all over England and Wales. We answer the questions twice; the first time in very simple language and the second time with more detail about the law, good practice and guidelines. Depending on the amount of information you require you can choose to read one, or both of these answers.

Putting it into practice
This section is designed for staff to use in practical settings: for example, with colleagues, managers or service users, in training, staff meetings or sessions. It brings together some resource materials that we use at **fpa** which we hope will be of use to you.

The law in more detail
This section is for those who wish to have more background information about the law in general or want some more details about the offences described in this publication. It may be useful for anyone intending to carry out training in this area, those developing policies and as a reference point to more detailed information.

A note about terminology in this publication

Learning disability
We use the term 'learning disability' throughout this publication. We acknowledge that there are variations of this term used in different areas of England and Wales.

Parent/carer
This term is always used when referring to the parents or the foster carers, or the adoptive parents of a person. This does not include professional carers who work with people with learning disabilities.

Client
'Client' is the term that we have chosen to use to describe people with learning disabilities that you work with. In this context 'client' is used in respect of someone who accesses a service and not someone who is dependent upon that service.

Inside this guide...

(continued)

Question

People with learning disabilities ... understanding the law on sex

Finding the right balance

Sex is a steamy subject. It gets people worried and excited at the same time. Sex is everywhere around us – in advertisements, films, television, newspapers and magazines – but somehow it is still hard to talk about it sensibly. There are so many different points of view that it appears very easy to upset someone by saying the wrong thing.

Sometimes we have to talk about sex because it is obviously an issue and if you work with people with learning disabilities there are some extra concerns. We have to support our clients to express their sexual feelings and identity, and protect them from exploitation and harm. Sexual abuse and exploitation of people with learning disabilities is widespread and easy to cover up, leaving people who are already vulnerable seriously harmed.

It is never easy to find the right mix between protection and supporting people to understand sexual activity and explore their sexual identity. Protecting people from all risks may seem like the safest thing in the short term, but can leave people more exposed to abuse and danger in the future. Parents/carers and support staff develop plans together that are hopefully right for each individual. Finding that combination of protection and support is just the same when it comes to people's sex lives. It can, however, seem like a much more complex task because it is such a sensitive area and you may be unsure whether there are laws which you have to take account of.

Legal framework

There are two factors here: there are some laws which set out a framework for what is right and wrong on sex and it is important that staff are aware of and understand these. But, at the same time, social and cultural influences, such as assumptions about people's ability to have sex, embarrassment and some mistaken ideas about the law often stop sex being properly addressed. A person may not want to be the first to raise something they find embarrassing, so sometimes sex and relationships education (SRE) is not provided even when it is needed. And if a new sexual relationship is developing some staff may think they should stop it and keep people apart in case anything goes wrong. People sometimes justify these mistakes by saying that they thought that people with learning disabilities are not allowed or do not need SRE.

Ability to make choices

These cautious approaches ignore the fact that SRE gives people real confidence, ability to make choices and, in turn, greater protection from exploitation. We all have a right to understand our bodies and feelings and to know what is appropriate and inappropriate sexual behaviour. The opportunity to develop loving sexual relationships is an important and valued part of adult life. This is why we have to support people's right to develop their sexuality as an integral part of their identity, but we need to do so in ways that are appropriate and legally sound.

In our experience as trainers who work with groups of staff (and parents/carers) to improve their confidence and awareness about sex, relationships and SRE, we find that everyone wants to start by being clear on what the law says is right or wrong. They can then go on and learn more about the subject, confident that they know where they stand and what they can and can't do.

Scope of this book

We have written this book for you as someone who supports people with learning disabilities to help you understand the law on sex.[1] This should help you with day-to-day support or when incidents arise, especially at times when there is no one available to consult. But we hope that you will also use the book as part of planning people's education and care, and to inform your local policies. Difficult incidents can be the result of lack of planning and preparation, and sexual incidents are no exception.

Publication of the first issue of this book coincided with major changes to the law about sexual offences, and people with learning disabilities were covered specifically in the new legislation. The laws, which are within the Sexual Offences Act 2003, intended to make it easier to prosecute and bring cases of abuse to court, so we wanted to help you interpret how the law applies in your own work environment. We also wanted to include how the law fits with policy, guidelines and any rules and expectations you may have around you in your work, so that

---

[1] The law described in this publication relates to England and Wales. All information was correct at the time of going to press.

you can understand where there may seem to be some conflicting pressures about what is the right thing to do.

The latest edition of this book contains all this information and clarifies the Mental Capacity Act 2005, which was just emerging when the previous edition was written. It also highlights the Mental Health Act 2007. Two new questions concerning sex between family members and how to prevent sexual offending in people with learning disabilities have been included. *No Secrets*, the Department of Health and Home Office guidance on developing and implementing multi-agency policies and products to protect vulnerable adults from abuse was under review at the time this edition was published.

fpa has run training for many years, and our courses always include coverage of the law, so we know the kinds of questions that people ask and the issues that they worry about. Staff have told us about hundreds of individual incidents and situations where they have been unsure of the legal position. We have considered these issues and situations and put together a list of the most common questions we have been asked, and used these to explain the law, without using too much legal jargon. For those of you who want or need more detail we also include references to the relevant parts of the legislation.

At the end of the book you will find some materials that could help you explain some of this to your colleagues, at team meetings or perhaps to parents'/carers' groups. We also include some additional resources and further reading which could be useful.

We have tried to make the main part of this book easy to read, so it can be used by as many people as possible. We hope that in addition to staff and managers in learning disability services others will find it useful, including parents/carers, advocates and clients themselves. We would welcome feedback on how well we have achieved this, so please write to **fpa** (see back page for address) to tell us how you get on, especially if there are situations we have not covered. We would particularly like to hear how things turn out if you use the book to help to change attitudes towards sexuality or if you have applied the new laws in practice.

The law and other rules we work with

In your working life there will be many (sometimes conflicting) pressures on you when you have to decide what is the right thing to do in supporting people with learning disabilities. Here we show how the law fits with some of the other rules around us.

International and European laws/rules

There are declarations of rights that apply to everybody including some especially for people with learning disabilities. Some of these rights have been brought into our national law, but others have no real power (see page 102 for an example).

National laws

This is what we mainly cover in this book. These come from Acts of Parliament (statute law), or from decisions made by judges and juries in court over the years (case law). The laws in England and Wales are often different from the laws in Scotland and in Northern Ireland.

Religious traditions/rules

If you are a member of a faith group there may be rules about how you live, for example about sexual behaviour or contraception. These can apply to members of faith groups wherever they are in the world if the members choose to opt into the rules (see **fpa**'s factsheet *Religion, contraception and abortion*).

Professional codes of conduct

Different professional groups have their own rules for their members: for example, most professions have strict rules about patient or client confidentiality.

Regional or local guidelines

These could include child protection procedures or guidelines for the protection of vulnerable adults. It is good practice to know about and work to these, where they exist.

Employers' policies and guidelines

These are not the same as employment law (which is legally binding). You could lose your job if you fail to keep to the policies and guidelines of your employer. Some employers have clear policies about sexual behaviour but others do not.

Local society's expectations

Break these rules and you could get stared at, shouted at or worse. For example, can people kiss in the street? What if they are the same sex? What if they are learning disabled? These rules are not written down but they affect people's lives significantly.

Family and cultural expectations

These rules are unwritten too, but can be even stronger. Anyone who is part of a family or cultural group has to behave in an acceptable way or risk being excluded. Disabled people may be excused some of these expectations but staff are expected to help people fit in to their culture as much as possible. People who move house or develop friendships can find that there are differences between the culture of their new friendship group and that of their family or home area.

House rules for individual workplaces or living places
Every workplace or living place will have written or unwritten rules: for example, rules about visitors, record keeping and acceptable behaviour.

Custom and practice of staff
"How we've always done things here" is often the most powerful rule of all! Many legal myths start out this way. People are often astonished to find that other places and people do things differently.

Clients' expectations
People get used to how other people behave around them, and can be surprised and worried when things change. New rules, ideas and ways of doing things take some time to adjust to, however good they are. People's expectations may differ from the culture of the service.

Usually these different types of rules will support each other but sometimes there may be conflict. You will make your own decisions about finding a path through the different pressures, but if it's not clear you must seek advice and support from your manager or from one of the organisations recommended throughout this publication.

Remember that if you keep good records, seek advice, and show that you have been doing your best at all times to do the right thing, then you are protecting yourself and people with learning disabilities that you work with and support. If in doubt, write everything down and get some help – you shouldn't have to struggle with this on your own.

Sex, the law and people with learning disabilities

This section contains answers to the most common questions asked about the law when we deliver training. The first response is a quick summary with no legal jargon or reference to legislation, written for people who want a clear and straightforward answer to their question. We hope the people with learning disabilities that you work with will be able to understand these answers, with some help from you, where appropriate.

We then go on to tell you what the law says about each situation. This is to provide support for people who want more detailed information, with explanations or the relevant legislation and references about where to go for more information.

We hope that this section is easy to follow and you can find the answers to your questions.

Are my clients allowed to have sex?

S ome people still think that people with learning disabilities either cannot or should not have sex. This attitude dates back to a time when sex was discouraged. In the past, people with learning disabilities were often seen as either like children, who would not be interested in sex, or as over-sexed and dangerous. Even though these ideas contradicted each other, they led to men and women being kept apart. There were also assumptions that people with learning disabilities could not be parents or that their children would also be disabled. Now that we respect people's full rights as adults, we understand that everyone develops sexual feelings even if they may not always be able to express them without support.

People with learning disabilities who are aged 16 and over have the same right to have sexual relationships as everybody else, as long as they are able to consent to different elements of a relationship. We should assume that everyone has this capacity, until it is proved otherwise. There is, however, some extra protection offered by the law, which is covered in some of the other questions in this book.

Of course, the right to have sex does not necessarily mean that someone can make this a reality, as they may not have the ability or the opportunity to form a relationship with a willing partner.

What the law, good practice and guidance say ...

It is legal for anyone aged 16 years and over to engage in consensual sexual activity with partners of the same or opposite sex. This applies to anyone with a learning disability provided the person has the capacity to consent to sexual activity.

The definition of consent within the Sexual Offences Act 2003 is as follows:

"A person consents if he agrees by choice and has the freedom and capacity to make that choice."

The issue of consent is covered in more detail in Question 2.

The Mental Capacity Act 2005 encourages people to optimise the capacity of people with learning disabilities and ensure that they are engaged in the decision making process. It is important to note that **no decision regarding sexual activity can be made on behalf of someone else** so some of the principles of the Mental Capacity Act can not apply in situations regarding sexual activity. However, some of the principles could be useful when considering people's life circumstances.

The principles (as outlined in the Mental Capacity Act) are:

- A person must be assumed to have capacity unless it is established that he lacks capacity.

- A person is not to be treated as unable to make a decision unless all practicable steps to help him to do so have been taken without success.

- A person is not to be treated as unable to make a decision merely because he makes an unwise decision.

- An act done, or decision made, under this Act for or on behalf of a person who lacks capacity must be done, or made, in his best interests.

- Before the act is done, or the decision is made, regard must be had to whether the purpose for which it is needed can be as effectively achieved in a way that is less restrictive of the person's rights and freedom of action.

[Mental Capacity Act 2005]

The Act looks at who lacks capacity. It focuses on the particular time when a decision has to be made and on the particular matter to which the decision relates, not on any theoretical ability to make decisions generally. It should not be presumed that someone who does not have the capacity to consent to one activity does not have the capacity to make any decisions. Each decision should be treated individually.

The Act sets out a test for assessing whether a person lacks capacity to take a particular decision at a particular time.

The test (as outlined in the Mental Capacity Act) is whether the person can:

- understand the information relevant to the decision

- retain that information

- use or weigh that information as part of the process of making the decision

- communicate his decision (whether by talking, using sign language or any other means).

[Mental Capacity Act 2005]

When we are looking at the issue of a client having sex, we should use the Sexual Offences Act definition to decide whether they are able to consent or not (this is explained in more detail in the next question). It is different from the definition of capacity in the Mental Capacity Act 2005.

Some people with learning disabilities may not be able to give consent to sexual activity at an age when other people can. They should be offered support, including education to enable them to give safe, informed consent. This will include supporting them to understand the nature of sexual activity and its consequences.

Further information

Department for Constitutional Affairs, Department of Health and Welsh Assembly Government, *Mental Capacity Act 2005 – Easy Read Summary* (Department of Health, 2006).

Department for Constitutional Affairs, Department of Health, Welsh Assembly Government and Public Guardianship Office, *Mental Capacity Act 2005 – Summary* (Department of Health, 2006).

Mental Capacity Act 2005 (see www.opsi.gov.uk).

What about my clients who cannot make choices for themselves?

People will often be able to consent to sex if they have had the chance to learn about it. Some people do not have enough understanding to be able to consent to sexual relationships. They may be able to do so in the future with some sex and relationships education, or they may never develop this ability. The law gives these people extra protection against abuse. It is illegal for anyone to have sex with someone who cannot consent to sexual activity.

Sometimes two people with learning disabilities have sex with each other, and both are unable to consent. If neither partner has the capacity to consent and neither is distressed or being exploited they will not be prosecuted, but you may need to take action to protect one or both of them (see Question 5 for more about your responsibilities in this situation).

What the law, good practice and guidance say ...

Everyone who is 16 and over is assumed to have the capacity to consent (see Question 1 for the definition of 'consent'). By that age they will generally have the knowledge and understanding to appreciate what sexual activity is, and any reasonable foreseeable consequences of that activity.

Most people with a learning disability can make many of their own decisions, including whether to engage in sexual activity. There will be some people who will not have a level of understanding which enables a particular decision to be made; therefore they may lack capacity in relation to some complex issues.

If two people have sex together but neither has the capacity to consent to sexual activity they will not be prosecuted under the offences of the Sexual Offences Act 2003. The Minister of State gave assurances on this point during the Lords committee stage of the Bill.

The Sexual Offences Act 2003 introduced a number of offences that provide protection to people with a mental disorder. The legislation uses the term 'people with a mental disorder' to include people with learning disabilities and people with mental health problems. This definition of 'mental disorder' comes from the Mental Health Act 1983 (see section 'The law in more detail', starting on page 111).

Some sections of the Sexual Offences Act 2003 deal with anybody with a mental disorder, but Sections 30–33 of the Act specifically deal with offences against persons with a mental disorder who are unable to choose or refuse sexual activity.

These Sections apply where sexual activity involves someone who does not have the capacity to choose whether to agree to that activity because:

● they lack sufficient understanding of the nature, or possible consequences of what happens

● or they are unable to communicate such a choice

● or for any other reason.

Even if someone is able to consent to most things, there may be circumstances in which they cannot make a choice. Someone's capacity to choose could be impeded, for instance, if they are unclear about the distinction between personal care and sexual activity (see Question 4); or did not understand the link between intercourse and pregnancy; or if they were unable to speak or make themselves understood to the perpetrator (the person carrying out the offence); or didn't know about sexually transmitted infections; or if they did not know that they were allowed to make a choice.

The sections of the Act covering offences against someone with a mental disorder who is unable to choose sexual activity use the idea that someone may be 'unable to refuse'.

The offences in detail are:

30: Sexual activity with a person with a mental disorder impeding choice

Sexual activity includes any form of intentional sexual touching, which can include penetration. This will cover many instances of abuse. The maximum sentence for this offence is life where penetration occurs, and 14 years in other cases.

31: Causing or inciting a person with a mental disorder impeding choice to engage in sexual activity

These cases could involve a third party, so the perpetrator could be inciting the person with a mental disorder to masturbate, or to have sex with, another person. The maximum sentence for this offence is life where penetration occurs, and 14 years in other cases.

32: Engaging in sexual activity in the presence of a person with a mental disorder impeding choice

This offence must be carried out for the sexual gratification of the perpetrator, and the perpetrator intends that the victim is aware of the sexual activity. The offence carries a maximum sentence of ten years.

33: Causing a person with a mental disorder impeding choice to watch a sexual act

Again, this offence must be carried out for the sexual gratification of the perpetrator and the sexual act can be live, filmed or in picture form. This would include images on computers or via web cams, and they can be produced by any means, so manufactured images (such as cartoons or computer graphics) would also be included. The offence carries a maximum sentence of ten years.

In these offences (and offences covered in Question 7 relating to inducements and so on), an offender must have known, or be reasonably expected to have known that the victim had a mental disorder, and that because of that disorder the victim was likely to be unable to refuse.

Other offences against persons with a mental disorder are covered in Sections 34–37 of the Act (see Question 7) and Sections 38–41 (see Question 9).

Sections 30–44 of the Sexual Offences Act 2003 cover offences and definitions relating to people with a mental disorder. The Act supersedes all previous legislation, particularly the Sexual Offences Act 1956. These offences:

● supersede the previous 'intercourse with a mental defective' offence: the term 'defective' is now removed from law

● increase the previous maximum sentence of one to two years, to a maximum of life

● are gender neutral: men with learning disabilities now have the same protection as women.

Further information

Home Office, *Adults: Safer from Sexual Crime – The Sexual Offences Act 2003* (Home Office Communications Directorate, 2004).

Murphy G, 'Capacity to consent to sexual relationships in adults with learning disabilities', *Journal of Family Planning and Reproductive Healthcare*, vol 29, no 3 (2003), 148–149.

3

What exactly is rape?

Rape is when a man puts his penis into someone's vagina, anus or mouth when that person does not agree (consent). It is the most serious sexual offence and has the strongest penalties.

For someone to agree to sexual activity they must be able to do so freely and with understanding. If your client does not have the capacity or freedom to choose sexual activity and someone has sex with them, the offence of rape has been committed.

Only a man or boy can commit rape as it has to be done with a penis. The legal age of responsibility is ten, so for rape to occur the man or boy must be aged ten or over. The person who is raped could be a man, a woman or a child, and could be someone who has had a sex change operation (a transsexual). The penis does not have to go in very far or for very long: any penetration is still rape. It is still rape if there is no ejaculation.

Sex that is penetration with a penis is always rape when the person it is happening to meets any one of the following criteria:

● does not consent to it at that time

● is under 13 (even if they say they consent)

● is too drunk or drugged or unwell to consent

● has a severe learning disability or other mental disorder that makes them unable to understand enough to consent.

Rape is the starting point for deciding about any sexual offence that includes penetration of someone's body. It may be that another offence is more appropriate, but that would only be accepted if it could be shown that it was not rape.

What the law, good practice and guidance say ...

Rape is defined as the intentional penetration with a penis of the vagina, anus or mouth of another person, without that person's consent.

[Sexual Offences Act 2003 Section 1]

This definition states that the act is carried out with someone who does not consent. The law then defines consent (see Question 1) as when someone agrees by choice and that this agreement must be freely given and can only be given where the individual has the capacity to choose. Therefore, if someone does not have the capacity to choose, the offence of rape has been committed. In addition, the law contains specific offences to better protect people with a learning disability.

This position clarifies that not consenting includes being unable to consent. The Home Office hopes that this will make it easier for people with learning disabilities to bring charges under these offences.

The definition of rape includes oral penetration (penetration of the mouth), and also includes surgically reconstructed genitalia (such as from a sex change operation). The Gender Recognition Act 2004 ensures that transsexuals can be recognised in law as the gender they have become.

Penetration does not need to include ejaculation. The offence is the violation of the victim, not the satisfaction of the perpetrator.

Rape can only be committed by a man, since it involves the use of the penis. If a woman were involved in carrying out a sexual attack that included rape of another person by a man, she could be charged under another offence such as 'Causing a person to engage in a sexual activity without consent' (see Question 4). Where such an offence involves penetration the maximum sentence can be the same as for rape, depending on the circumstances.

There is no marriage exemption to a rape offence. A husband is guilty of rape if he has non-consensual sex with his wife.

[Sexual Offences (Amendment) Act 1992]

Further information

Voice UK, *Stop! No More Abuse* (Voice UK, 2003).

Rape and Sexual Abuse Support Centre
Support and counselling for women and girls who have been raped or sexually abused. Also provides a referral service for men.
Helpline: 020 8683 3300 (minicom: 020 8239 1124)
www.rasasc.org.uk

Rape Crisis
Offers resources and information to survivors of sexual violence and their friends and families, and signposts rape crisis support groups around the country.
www.rapecrisis.org.uk

Respond
Provides a range of services to both victims and perpetrators of sexual abuse who have learning disabilities. Support for families, carers and professionals is also provided.
Tel: 020 7383 0700
www.respond.org.uk

Survivors UK
Support, counselling and local groups for male survivors of any kind of sexual violence or rape, plus training for professionals.
Helpline: 0845 122 1201
www.survivorsuk.org.uk

Voice UK
Provides telephone support for adults and children with learning disabilities who have been abused, and for their families and carers.
Helpline: 0845 122 8695
www.voiceuk.org.uk

What about other forced sexual activity?

A ny sort of sexual touching is against the law if the person it is done to does not consent. Some of the offences involved are still very serious, even if they are not rape. The most serious ones involve penetrating someone's vagina or anus with objects or with other parts of the body such as fingers. But any sexual touching is sexual assault if someone does not agree to it. It is also against the law to make someone do sexual things, even if they are not being touched (for example, making them touch themselves or other people in a sexual way).

What the law, good practice and guidance say ...

If someone does not consent to sexual activity, the perpetrator could be charged with one of the non-consensual offences. As well as rape (covered in Question 3), there are three of these offences and they can apply to anyone. These offences can apply if the victim has learning disabilities, although there are other more specific offences to further protect people with learning disabilities in cases where a person is unable to consent freely (see Question 2).

The offences are:

● sexual assault

● assault by penetration

● causing a person to engage in sexual activity without consent.

The Sexual Offences Act 2003 changed the definition of the first offence, and introduced the other two for the first time.

The basis of these offences is that the victim does not freely consent to an activity. This means that the victim is unable to refuse the sexual activity. This could be for a number of reasons, including that the victim:

● was drugged, drunk, asleep or unconscious

● was threatened with, or subject to violence

● was encouraged to believe that the sexual activity was a care activity

- was unable to communicate because of a physical disability
- was kidnapped at the time of the act.

A defendant charged with one of these offences would need to demonstrate that he had a reasonable belief that consent was given, and produce evidence to support this belief.

[Sexual Offences Act 2003]

Sexual assault

This is explained in detail in Question 8.

Assault by penetration

It is an offence to intentionally penetrate the vagina or anus of someone else with any part of the body or with an object, if the penetration is sexual and the person does not consent.

The insertion of another body part (for example, finger) or an object (for example, bottle, vibrator or weapon) could cause as much fear or distress and potentially worse internal injuries than penile rape.

This offence might also be used where the victim is unsure what they were penetrated with and could not say with certainty that they were raped with a penis.

This new offence can be committed by both males and females, and the maximum sentence is life.

Causing a person to engage in sexual activity without consent

This offence *[Sexual Offences Act 2003 Section 4]* covers any kind of sexual activity without consent where the perpetrator does not directly sexually assault the victim. For instance, it would apply to a woman who forces a man to penetrate her, or a perpetrator who makes a victim engage in masturbation or makes two victims have sex with each other. It could be used in the case of a woman holding another woman down while she is raped.

Further information

See Question 3.

How much is it my responsibility to make sure my clients are consenting to sexual activity?

If you discover or believe that a client is involved in sexual activity, you may not know if what they are doing is fully consenting and wonder whether you should stop it. Sometimes staff are concerned about whether the sex the client is having is legal or illegal. These are two separate questions.

First and foremost, you have a duty of care to protect your client or another vulnerable person from harm, so if you think your client is being abused or exploited you must intervene to stop this from happening. If the incident is happening now, then do what you can to stop it right away including talking to a manager or other colleague about the situation. If it is not happening now, get advice from your manager about the best way to protect your client in the future. Serious legal claims could be made against you for not following your duty of care, and it is your duty to do everything you can to make sure that your client is not abused or exploited while protecting their rights. (See Question 9 when the sexual activity involves a client and care worker.)

Deciding whether any abuse or exploitation is happening may not always be a clear cut matter. It may be unclear whether someone understands sex and its consequences, and if there is not sufficient understanding there cannot be consent. If you are in any doubt as to whether a client is consenting, you must get advice.

People can be helped to understand sex and its consequences through education and counselling and this may be an ongoing process.

What the law, good practice and guidance say ...

You have an obligation to exercise a level of care towards an individual, as is reasonable in all the circumstances, to avoid injury to that individual or his/her property. This is called a duty of care which means that someone who has more knowledge and/or experience than someone else has to make sure that their actions do not cause the other person harm, either to their person or their property. There is no actual written contract over the action, but a complaint could be made and compensation given if a member of staff or an organisation does not abide by their duty of care to their clients.

You don't have to cause loss or harm deliberately. A breach of duty of care is where you are negligent, where you could reasonably have foreseen what could happen.

A negligent act is an unintentional but careless act that results in loss. Only a negligent act will be regarded as having breached a duty of care.

Duty of care is a common law duty, which means it has been established by court decisions rather than by an Act of Parliament. Liability for breach of a duty of care very much depends on the public policy at the time the case is heard.

The only law-breaking that there is an obligation to report is where you know or suspect that some terrorist act is being committed or planned. You also have to report any harm or danger of harm to children. So you are not committing any offence if you decide not to report illegal sexual activity involving adults if you believe it to be consenting and not abusive or exploitative. But it is possible that your employer has a policy on this, and you may have to record and report it as part of your conditions of employment.

Further information

See How **fpa** can help you and **fpa** publications and resources in the Bibliography – both at the end of this book.

Thompson D and Brown H, *Response-ability: Working with Men with Learning Disabilities who have Abusive or Unacceptable Behaviour* (Mental Health Foundation, 1999).

UNISON, *The Duty of Care* (UNISON Communications, 2003).

6

I work with teenage clients with learning disabilities. How old do they have to be before they can legally have sex?

The age of consent for any form of sexual activity, not just sexual penetration, is 16. This is the same for everybody, including partners of the same sex. Anybody who has sex with someone under the age of 16 is breaking the law, even if they are under-age themselves. Penalties are especially serious for sex with children under 13. These crimes are also dealt with more seriously if they are committed by someone over 18.

If there is no abuse or exploitation involved then there may be no good reason to bring legal charges in the case of sex between young people of similar ages: there is discretion for the Crown Prosecution Service to take all the circumstances into account.

The average age at first heterosexual intercourse is 16 for men and women.[2] Disabled young people, including those who are learning disabled, may not have any sexual experience until a later age – but some will. Disabled young people may be especially vulnerable to sexual abuse, and some will experience unwanted sexual activity at a young age.

Make sure you understand how and when you might have to take child protection action if you work with anyone aged under 18. You do not have a responsibility to report underage sex unless there is abuse or exploitation, or an organisation's policy or employment contract requires it.

What the law, good practice and guidance say ...

The age of consent for any sexual activity is 16 for same sex and opposite sex couples. The age of consent for sexual activity between men was equalised in 2000.

[Sexual Offences (Amendment) Act 2000]

Sexual activity is illegal with someone under 16, although if the young person is 13, 14 or 15 years old there may be a defence of 'reasonable belief' where the

---

[2] Wellings K, 'Sexual behaviour in Britain: early heterosexual experience', *Lancet*, vol 358 (2001) 1843–1850.

defendant would have to prove that he/she believed that the young person was aged 16 or over. For a young person aged 12 or under, this defence would not apply as anyone under the age of 13 is deemed as not having capacity to consent in legal terms. It is an absolute offence to have sex with someone under the age of 13, therefore it is likely that an adult defendant would have a non-consensual charge brought against them if the other party was under 13, regardless of consent.

For male offenders this could be:

- rape
- assault by penetration
- sexual assault
- causing a person to engage in sexual intercourse.

For female offenders the last three could apply.

[Sexual Offices Act 2003 Section 7]

The defendant could be anyone over ten, which is the age of criminal responsibility. The Crown Prosecution Service decides if prosecution is in the public interest. If the defendant was under 18, the situation would be assessed with regard to the age and emotional maturity of the parties and whether there was any element of corruption.

Further information

See How **fpa** can help you and **fpa** publications and resources in the Bibliography – both at the end of this book.

Davies L, *The Social Worker's Guide to Children and Families Law* (Jessica Kingsley Publishers, 2008).

Department for Children, Schools and Families, *Safeguarding Children and Young People from Sexual Exploitation. Draft Guidance* (Department for Children, Schools and Families, 2008).

Department for Children, Schools and Families, *Working Together to Safeguard Children: A Guide to Inter-agency Working to Safeguard and Promote the Welfare of Children* (Department for Children, Schools and Families, 2006).

Children's Legal Centre
The Children's Legal Centre produces a useful guide called *At What Age Can I?*
Tel: 01206 872 466
www.childrenslegalcentre.com

Crown Prosecution Service

The Crown Prosecution Service has produced guidance on the Sexual Offences Act 2003, specifically where both partners are consenting but under the age of consent.
Tel: 020 7796 8000
www.cps.gov.uk

My clients are more vulnerable than other people. Are there special laws about them being bribed or tricked into having sex?

Even if somebody says yes to sex, it may be because they have been tricked, bribed or threatened. They may not realise that sex in return for a favour or a cigarette is exploitation. If another person encourages them to have sex by saying that "All friends have sex, you have to do this with me" they may not realise that this is abusive and illegal. Someone with a learning disability could be very scared or worried about a threat that other people would know not to take seriously. Sometimes people with learning disabilities are shown pornography and told that it shows that this kind of sexual behaviour is what everyone does. This unwanted exposure to pornographic material can be very damaging.

The law makes it illegal to trick, bribe or threaten anyone with a learning disability or other mental disorder into any kind of sexual activity, even if they are people who are able to consent or make choices for themselves.

There is also an offence which is aimed at protecting young people who are being tricked or prepared by an adult for sexual purposes. Cases of this happening over the internet, where an adult may pretend to be a young person to get the trust of the victim, have increased in recent years. This is called grooming and it is often the way that paedophiles (adults who are sexually attracted to children) gain the trust of children and young people. However, it does not always involve the internet.

What the law, good practice and guidance say ...

Someone coercing another person into sexual activity by inducement, threat or deception (can be called suggestibility or compliance) could be dealt with by one or more of these four offences:

34: **Inducement, threat or deception to procure sexual activity with a person with a mental disorder.**

35: **Causing a person with a mental disorder to engage in, or agree to engage in sexual activity by inducement, threat or deception.**

36: **Engaging in sexual activity in the presence, procured by inducement, threat or deception, of a person with a mental disorder.**

37: **Causing a person with a mental disorder to watch a sexual act by inducement, threat or deception.**

[Sexual Offences Act 2003 Sections 34–37]

Inducements could include giving gifts or money, or promising presents or marriage to the victim. Deception could include telling lies such as "All your friends do this" or "You will get ill if you don't". Threats might include "I'll tell your parents" or "I'll hurt your friend".

These offences apply to people who are capable of deciding whether to engage in sexual activity, but whose agreement in a particular activity is improperly obtained. They also apply to people who cannot consent to sexual activity.

These offences are dealt with seriously and sentencing is up to life (where penetration occurs) for Sections 34 and 35, and up to ten years for Sections 36 and 37.

The offence which covers child grooming (all children under 16, not just those with learning disabilities) relates to:

Meeting a child following sexual grooming etc

[Sexual Offences Act 2003 Section 15]

This offence would be carried out if the defendant is an adult who has communicated at least twice with a young person. It is not necessary that these communications are sexual, and they can be in any form, although will often start in chat rooms on the internet. The offence is committed when the adult meets, or is travelling to meet the young person with the intention of committing a sexual offence against them. The offence carries a maximum of ten years' imprisonment.

Further information

www.ceop.gov.uk
The Child Exploitation and Online Protection (CEOP) Centre is part of the UK police force and is dedicated to protecting children from sexual abuse wherever they may be. The website contains lots of advice for parents, carers and young people.

www.iwf.org.uk
The Internet Watch Foundation is working with the Internet industry, police and Government to combat images of child abuse online.

QUESTION 8

Is it against the law for a client to grope me, or grope another client?

Groping is sexual assault. Some staff may report that parts of their body such as their breasts, genitals or bottom are groped or grabbed at by their clients. Some staff tell us that they are expected to put up with this as a normal and inevitable part of their work. Clients may also grope other clients or even members of the public, in shops or on the street or perhaps at home.

Sometimes this is because the clients genuinely do not know that this is wrong, or may not appreciate boundaries of what is or is not acceptable. Often it is because it has not been taken seriously enough for consistent work to be done towards stopping it happening.

Groping is still sexual even if the person who did it didn't really mean it to be sexual. This means that it is important that clients learn that they shouldn't do it, so they do not get into trouble. It is also important that staff (or other people) should not have to put up with being assaulted. You have a right to work in a safe place, and you must record and report these assaults and find out what your employer plans to do to prevent them and support you as the person who has been groped. It is your employer's responsibility to sort this out: it may be that they would need to change shifts or staffing in a service if your safety cannot be assured. Employers could be liable for not doing everything possible to provide a safe working environment.

It is also against the law for someone (client or staff) to watch someone else (client or staff) while they are bathing, going to the toilet or getting dressed, if they do it on purpose and are sexually excited by it. This can happen in residential or day services without clients knowing it is wrong.

What the law, good practice and guidance say ...

Sexual assault *[Sexual Offences Act 2003 Section 3]* supersedes the prior offences of Indecent assault (on a woman) and Indecent assault (on a man) *[Sexual Offences Act 1956]*. The maximum sentence for sexual assault is ten years.

This offence covers any kind of intentional sexual touching of somebody else without their consent. It includes touching (sexually) any part of their body, clothed or unclothed, either with any part of the body or with an object.

An activity is sexual if a reasonable person would either always consider it to be sexual because of its nature, for example oral sex, or if it would be considered sexual depending on the circumstances and intention. For example, a medical examination in a doctor's surgery, where the purpose is not sexual, would not be considered an assault.

Because of this wide definition proving sexual intent would not be necessary, just the intent to touch and the fact that the touch is sexual. These may be important elements to remember when teaching people with learning disabilities about appropriate and inappropriate touch, or when considering a disclosure of abuse.

It is often difficult for the person being touched, particularly if they are a member of staff, to report this, even if it is causing great distress. Staff may feel that they do not want their client to get into trouble, and that the touching is not serious anyway. Staff should not be put into a position where they feel intimidated by or uncomfortable with a client. It is not that staff member's role to make a decision about the actions to be taken. All sexual touching must be reported and recorded so that a manager can decide on the best course of action. Staff who do not report it are making their clients more vulnerable to getting in to trouble for doing it to someone else.

Under common law your employer has to provide a safe working environment for you. If they do not, they could be liable for claims of negligence.

[Health and Safety at Work Act 1974 Section 2]

There are often additional codes of practice for employers which will cover this as well. These will differ depending on the sector you work in.

Watching someone else while they are doing something in private is covered by an offence called Voyeurism *[Sexual Offences Act 2003]*. This is the covert observation, for the sexual gratification of oneself or others, of another person engaged in an activity of an intimate or personal nature, in circumstances where the person observed has a reasonable expectation of privacy. This offence could apply to staff and clients and in a wide range of settings, especially in residential accommodation.

Further information

Thompson D, Clare I C H and Brown H, 'Not such an "ordinary" relationship: the role of women support staff in relation to men with learning disabilities who have difficult sexual behaviour', *Disability and Society*, vol 12, no 4 (1997) 573–592.

QUESTION 9

One of my colleagues is having sex with a client. Is this wrong?

Care workers are in a position of trust in relation to those they care for and some carry out care of an intimate nature. Sometimes close relationships form between carers and clients which can be exploitative even if they appear to be innocent and genuine, such as when a client has a crush on a member of staff which bolsters their own self-esteem at the expense of the client. Because of the power difference between staff and clients, it is never safe to allow these relationships to become sexual. The law says that these relationships are wrong.

It is against the law for anyone involved in the care of anybody with a learning disability or other mental disorder to have any kind of sexual activity with them. The law defines 'care worker' widely. This includes anyone providing services and those in regular face-to-face contact with the client. This can include paid staff and volunteers or for example cleaners in residential homes or bus/taxi drivers.

If the partners were married or already in a relationship before one started to care for the other, then that is an exception to this, and the relationship can legally continue.

If a new genuine relationship develops between a care worker and a person with a learning disability who is able to consent, then the member of staff would need to move to a job which involves no working contact with the client or involvement in his or her care.

What the law, good practice and guidance say ...

It is an offence for care workers to engage in any form of sexual activity with the people that they care for.

Care workers

The definition of 'care worker' is wide to ensure that it includes all those who may have a duty of care towards clients.

Workers from care/community/voluntary/children's homes

This covers the full range of care accommodation someone with a mental disorder might find themselves in when not at home or in a hospital.

[Sexual Offences Act 2003 Section 42(5)]

Workers from NHS services or independent medical agencies

This includes workers from all NHS or private hospitals, walk-in centres, outpatient clinics, general practices and consulting rooms.

People in regular face-to-face contact with the client, providing services in connection with client's mental disorder, regardless of whether they provide physical or mental care

As well as 'traditional care staff' this definition also includes advocates, supervisors, alternative therapists and others providing forms of care. It also includes staff such as cleaners, gardeners, drivers and caretakers who have regular face-to-face contact with a client.

Paid or unpaid, full- or part-time

Offences in this area previously only referred to employed staff. This definition now includes volunteers as well as paid staff, and is effective regardless of how many hours they work.

It is anticipated that in cases tried under these offences the victim is more likely to have complied with this activity due to the relationship and trust they have with their care worker. This compliance, brought about by the position of trust held by the care worker, is not the same as free consent.

The offences are the same in description as the Sexual Offences Act 2003, Sections 30–33 (see Question 2) and Sections 34–37 (see Question 7), the perpetrator being a care worker.

38: Care workers: sexual activity with a person with a mental disorder

Sexual activity includes any form of intentional sexual touching, which can include penetration. The maximum sentence for this offence is 14 years where penetration occurs, and ten years in other circumstances.

39: Care workers: causing or inciting sexual activity

These cases could involve a third party, so the perpetrator could be inciting the person with a mental disorder to masturbate or have sex with another person. The maximum sentence for this offence is 14 years where penetration occurs, and ten years in other circumstances.

40: Care workers: sexual activity in the presence of a person with a mental disorder

This offence must be carried out for the sexual gratification of the perpetrator, and the perpetrator intends that the victim is aware of the sexual activity. The maximum sentence for this offence is seven years.

41: Care workers: causing a person with a mental disorder to watch a sexual act

This offence could include making someone watch a sexual act, either live or filmed or showing someone photographic or drawn images of sexual activity.

This offence is committed where the care worker gains sexual gratification. The maximum sentence for this offence is seven years.

It is not intended that this Section should prevent care workers from providing legitimate sex and relationships education, which ensures that, for example a care worker showing a person with a mental disorder in their care a video of a sexual act as part of an approved care plan (with their consent) will not be liable for this offence.

The perpetrator of these offences must be reasonably expected to know that the victim has a learning disability. The defendant will not be guilty if they have no knowledge of the client's learning disability, which would be unlikely if they were in a position represented above.

There are two exceptions to the care worker offence:

The marriage exception

No offence under Sections 38–41 of the Sexual Offences Act 2003 can be committed where a couple are lawfully married. This exception exists as the offences could cover voluntary care arrangements within a marriage where one partner cares for the other. Other sexual offences would still stand within marriage however.

The pre-existing relationship exception

No offence is committed where there was a pre-existing sexual relationship between a couple where one has subsequently become the carer for the other.

POVA

POVA is the Protection of Vulnerable Adults scheme. It is included within the Care Standards Act 2000. Implementation of POVA began in July 2004.

The main aim of the scheme is the introduction of the POVA list where care workers who have harmed a vulnerable adult, or placed a vulnerable adult at risk of harm, will be banned from working in a care position.

This currently covers care workers in care homes and those working within people's own homes. It also covers employment agencies, businesses which supply the care workers and adult placement schemes.

All prospective employees will be checked to ensure they are not on the list as part of the Criminal Records Bureau Disclosure application process.

People with learning disabilities working as volunteers

Many organisations for people with learning disabilities use volunteers who have learning disabilities themselves and may be clients of the service. These staff can be classified as care workers under the Sexual Offences Act 2003. Therefore, if they form relationships with other clients the same offences could apply to them. Organisations must address this issue in their policies and ensure that volunteers are aware of this before genuine, consensual relationships are formed.

Further information

Department of Health, *Protection of Vulnerable Adults (POVA) Scheme in England and Wales for Care Homes and Domiciliary Care Agencies: A Practical Guide* (Department of Health, 2006).

Department of Health and Home Office, *No Secrets: Guidance on Developing and Implementing Multi-agency Policies and Procedures to Protect Vulnerable Adults from Abuse* (Department of Health and Home Office Communications Directorate, 2000).

10

What should I do if I think a colleague is abusing a client?

A t work, a member of staff may witness behaviour between a client and a colleague or manager that they do not feel is appropriate.

This is a very difficult situation as reporting a colleague (sometimes called whistle blowing) can be very stressful. Reporting the behaviour of a manager can be even more difficult and staff often do not know who to speak to or whether what they have seen is serious enough to report.

But if you are concerned about the behaviour of a fellow staff member or a manager you *must* report them. If they are causing a client harm in any way it is your duty to discuss this with someone and it would be a breach of your duty of care if you did not take action. It might also lead to you losing your job if you do not report them.

You must report the activity to your line manager, unless it is your line manager that you have concerns about, in which case you should go to the person who manages your manager or the regulatory body for your profession. Never approach the person yourself or try to deal with the situation without reporting it.

If you cannot speak to your line manager, you could see if your organisation has a whistle blowing policy and follow the guidance in that or approach one of the organisations listed in this section. There is law which safeguards your actions in this situation.

If you are a member of a union at work talk to your union representative. They will be able to support you in your actions and can also be contacted for advice.

What the law, good practice and guidance say ...

If you know of an action which is causing a client harm, you have a common law duty of care to report this, and to ensure that your client is safe (see Question 5 for more information about duty of care). This can be difficult when it is a colleague, or perhaps a manager causing harm to the client, but you must deal with it.

Organisations should have a whistle blowing policy which supports staff in this situation, and this should be the first thing you refer to. The proposed action should be to go immediately to your line manager with your concern. However, in some situations this may not be possible or appropriate so you should speak with another colleague or contact an organisation that can help you.

Most areas have a local safeguarding adults team who will be able to help in situations such as these. The regulatory body for your profession will be an organisation which maintains the standards within your profession and can provide advice and support in a situation such as this.

The Public Interest Disclosure Act 1998 (which amended the Employment Rights Act 1996) safeguards staff disclosing information so that employment cannot be taken away due to the reporting of an incident where someone is breaking the law or someone is being hurt.

Further information

Calcraft R and Ann Craft Trust, *Blowing the Whistle on Abuse of Adults with Learning Disabilities* (Ann Craft Trust, 2005).

Ann Craft Trust, The
An organisation that works with staff in the statutory, independent and voluntary sectors to protect people with learning disabilities who may be at risk from abuse. It also provides advice and information to parents and carers who have concerns about someone that they are supporting.
Tel: 0115 951 5400
www.anncrafttrust.org

Care and Social Services Inspectorate Wales (CSSIW)
Encourages the improvement of social care, early years and social services in Wales.
Tel: 01443 848 450
www.cssiw.org.uk

Care Quality Commission
Regulates health and adult social care services provided by the NHS, local authorities, private companies and voluntary organisations. Also protects the rights of people held under the Mental Health Act.
Tel: 03000 616161
www.cqc.org.uk

Public Concern at Work
An independent charity that operates a free, confidential legal helpline to advise workers on whether or how to raise concerns about danger or illegality that they witness at work (whistle blowing). It also advises and assists organisations with risk management and setting up whistle blowing policies to allow them to address staff concerns appropriately.
Tel: 020 7404 6609
www.pcaw.co.uk

Trades Union Congress (TUC)
The TUC represents working people from all walks of life and campaigns for a fair deal at work and for social justice at home and abroad.
Tel: 020 7636 4030
www.tuc.org.uk

Is it legal for my client to have sex with someone in the same family? Does it make any difference if they are both adults?

It is against the law to engage in any sexual activity with family members, regardless of whether they are children or adults; although the punishment would be less severe if both are adults (over 18). Sexual activity between family members is sometimes called incest, even though the law does not call it this any more.

The law forbids sexual activity between parent (including step-parent or adoptive parent) and child, and between grandparent and grandchild. Additionally, any adult living with a child or young person (under 18) for whom they have a significant caring role, may not have sex with them – even if the young person is 16 or 17 years old. Sex with a brother or sister (or half-brother or half-sister) is against the law. An uncle or aunt may not have sex with a niece or nephew, but cousins may legally have sex.

The same laws that protect children and vulnerable people still apply as well.

What the law, good practice and guidance say...

If you suspect that a client's family member is engaging in sexual activity with them you must report it to social services as a child protection concern (if the client is under 18) or as a protection of a vulnerable adult concern. Any form of sexual activity between certain family members is illegal.

The Sexual Offences Act 2003 states that the following are illegal:

● any form of sexual activity with a child family member

● any form of enticing a child family member to engage in sexual activity.

These offences apply whether or not the child has a learning disability.

A family member is described as: parent (including adoptive parents), grandparent, brother, sister, half-brother, half-sister, aunt or uncle, or someone who is, or has been, a foster parent.

The laws also apply if the two people live in the same household and one is regularly involved in caring for, training, supervising or being in sole charge of the other. Where two people live together and one cares for the other this could include step-parents (including partners who are not married), a cousin, stepbrother or stepsister, or a situation where the parent or foster parent of one person is, or has been, the other person's foster parent.

There are two exceptions to these offences. One is where the people involved are over 16 and legally married. The other is where the sexual relationship existed before the family relationship. For example, if two people meet because their respective 16- and 17-year-old children are engaged in a sexual relationship, and the parents decide to marry and all four move into the same household, the criminal law would not interfere in the ongoing sexual relationship between the children, even though they would otherwise have been brought within the scope of the offence.

For family members engaging in sexual activity with adults with learning disabilities the learning disability offences (see Questions 1, 4 and 7) would apply where the client does not, or can not consent to the sexual activity. If they do consent there are two additional offences which could apply:

● Sex with an adult relative: penetration.

● Sex with an adult relative: consenting to penetration.

Adoptive relatives are excluded from this offence but it is illegal for all other adult relatives to have sex with each other during which they penetrate each other or consent to be penetrated.

Further information

National Association of People Abused in Childhood (NAPAC)
Support and information for people abused in childhood.
Helpline: 0800 085 330
www.napac.org.uk

Stop it now!
A public information and awareness raising campaign.
Helpline: 0808 1000 900
www.stopitnow.org.uk

Should my clients be taught about sex and relationships?

Most people receive sex and relationships education (SRE) (of varying quality) while they are at school. People with learning (and other) disabilities often miss out. This may be because teachers and/or parents/carers think they will not need it, or it may be needed at a developmental stage that is later than the school age at which it is provided.

Legally, everyone has a right to SRE in the science curriculum while in school, whatever their abilities. After school age, there are no rights to this education, but it is good practice to make sure an educational needs assessment is part of a client's individual plan. Clients who have not had sex and relationships education are much more vulnerable to abuse by other people, to the danger of abusing or offending others, and to unplanned pregnancy or sexually transmitted infections from unsafe sex. Care providers could be at risk of a breach of duty of care for not providing this education at appropriate stages in people's lives.

Sometimes SRE for people with learning disabilities needs to be more explicit and detailed than mainstream SRE. This is often because it is being provided to adults rather than children, but also because the language and images have to be very clear and unambiguous. SRE can be responsive, such as answering questions or discussing situations as they arise, or it can be a planned programme or, ideally, a combination of the two. You must make sure that any explicit materials are part of an agreed plan which sets out who should be delivering it. Work of this kind with people with learning disabilities needs to be flexible and repeated as many times as necessary.

What the law, good practice and guidance say ...

Legal framework for SRE in England

The Education Act 1996 consolidated all previous legislation, and key points related to SRE are:

- The sex education elements of the National Curriculum Science Order are mandatory for all pupils of primary and secondary school age. These cover anatomy, puberty, biological aspects of sexual reproduction and use of hormones to control and promote fertility.

- Secondary schools are required to provide an SRE programme which includes (as a minimum) information about sexually transmitted infections and HIV.

- Other elements of personal, social and health education (PSHE), including SRE, are non-statutory.

- All schools must provide, and make available for inspection, an up-to-date policy describing the content and organisation of SRE outside of national curriculum science. This is the school governors' responsibility.

- Primary schools should have a policy statement that describes the SRE provided or gives a statement of the decision not to provide SRE.

- Following a review[3], the Government announced in October 2008 that comprehensive SRE will be made compulsory as a part of a statutory PSHE curriculum.[4]

The Learning and Skills Act 2000 requires that:

- Young people learn about the nature of marriage and its importance for family life and bringing up children.

- Young people are protected from teaching and materials which are inappropriate, having regard to the age and the religious and cultural background of the pupils concerned.

- School governing bodies have regard for the guidance.

- Parents have the right to withdraw their child from all or part of SRE provided outside national curriculum science.

---

[3] Review of Sex and Relationships Education (SRE) in Schools. A Report by the External Steering Group (2008).
[4] Department for Children, Schools and Families, *Government Response to the Report by the Sex and Relationships Education (SRE) Review Steering Group* (DCSF, 2008).

Legal framework for SRE in Wales

Under the Education Act 2002, SRE became a compulsory part of the basic curriculum in all secondary schools. Primary schools are also required to have a policy on SRE, outlining details of their SRE programme or explaining their decision not to provide SRE. The Welsh Assembly Government recommends that primary schools have a graduated programme of SRE tailored to the age and emotional maturity of the children.

Personal and social education (PSE) became a compulsory part of the basic curriculum in both primary and secondary schools in September 2003.[5] Schools are expected to base their provision of SRE and PSE on guidance produced by the Welsh Assembly Government.

The Sex and Relationships Education Guidance (DfEE, 2000) states that:

> "Mainstream schools and special schools have a duty to ensure that children with special educational needs and learning difficulties are properly included in sex and relationship education. Sex and relationship education should help all pupils understand their physical and emotional development and enable them to make positive decisions in their lives."

There are no laws relating to the provision of SRE outside formal education. However, there are many values and belief statements supporting the rights of people with learning disabilities to receive education in this area. One issue that often arises is that adult clients in less formal settings may never have had any form of SRE and this needs to be provided to ensure the safety and empowerment of that individual.

One proposed right is:

> "The right to be informed about sexuality and its place in human life, at times and at a level that allows this area of human being and experience to be as positive as possible."[6]

Keep up to date with changes in legislation by reading **fpa**'s factsheets *Sex and relationships education* and *Relationships and sexuality education* at www.fpa.org.uk.

---

[5] National Assembly for Wales, *Personal and Social Education (PSE) and Work-Related Education (WRE) in the Basic Curriculum, Circular 13/03* (National Assembly for Wales, 2003).

[6] Fairbairn G, Rowley D and Bowen M, *Sexuality, Learning Difficulties and Doing What's Right* (David Fulton Publishers, 1995).

Further information

See How **fpa** can help you and **fpa** publications and resources in the Bibliography – both at the end of this book.

Department for Children, Education, Lifelong Learning and Skills, *Personal and Social Education Framework for 7 to 19 Year Olds in Wales* (Welsh Assembly Government, 2008).

Department for Education and Employment, *Sex and Relationships Education Guidance, Circular 0116/2000* (Department for Education and Employment, 2000).

Fairbairn G, Rowley D and Bowen M, *Sexuality, Learning Difficulties and Doing What's Right* (David Fulton Publishers, 1995).

McCarthy M and Thompson D, *Sex and the 3 Rs: Rights, Responsibilities and Risks* (Pavilion Publishing, 1998).

National Assembly for Wales, *Sex and Relationships Education in Schools: Circular 11/02* (National Assembly for Wales, 2002).

Sex Education Forum, *Forum Factsheet 32, Sex and Relationships Education for Children and Young People with Learning Disabilities* (Sex Education Forum, 2004).

Sex Education Forum
The Sex Education Forum (part of the National Children's Bureau) is the national authority on sex and relationships education.
Tel: 020 7843 1901
www.ncb.org.uk/sef

Do I have to get the permission of the client's parents/carers before I provide sex and relationships education?

Both children and adults with learning disabilities will need sex and relationships education (SRE) at different stages in their lives. Sometimes this is arranged for everybody, and sometimes special programmes are developed for individuals. Staff may be unsure about whether they need parental permission to provide SRE for adult clients. Parental permission is not needed, but some staff have told us that they worry that parents/carers will object to SRE being provided and that if it goes ahead then the client could be withdrawn from the service completely. It is important to be sensitive to cultural and religious issues.

Supportive parents/carers can play a vital role in SRE by reinforcing the learning within the home for their son or daughter if the client wants them to do so.

Children at school have some SRE which is a compulsory part of the national curriculum within science lessons. Parents/carers are informed about this but cannot withdraw their children from the lessons. Additional SRE is usually also provided which is not part of the compulsory curriculum: parents/carers can withdraw their children from this if they are not happy about it.

Once people leave school there is no compulsory SRE, so people only receive whatever SRE is arranged by the college, day centre or support services they attend. Parents/carers do not have to be informed about this or give approval; however, in practice, it is usually a good idea to involve parents/carers or family so that educational messages can be consistent and reinforced at home with your client's consent.

However, you must be careful to support the client's confidentiality if the education is being provided because of particular circumstances in the client's life, such as a new relationship. Your client has a right to privacy, so you must not tell parents/carers personal information about the client without the client's consent.

It can come as a shock to some parents/carers to suddenly be told that their son or daughter is about to have SRE, so it is easier to let all parents/carers know as early as possible that this is a standard part of the service for everyone. In law, parents/carers have no say over what services are made available to an adult son or daughter. In practice, parents/carers could take their son or daughter to another service or move to another area, so co-operation is always best.

What the law, good practice and guidance say ...

If SRE is provided in school, parents/carers are informed about the provision. Parents/carers have the right to withdraw children from all parts of SRE provided outside the compulsory science curriculum.

When working with adults there is no legal requirement to inform their parents/carers when carrying out SRE. Sometimes, because of the nature of the work, you may feel that the involvement of the parents/carers would be beneficial. Supportive parents/carers can work in partnership with staff to ensure that everyone is sending the same messages to the client which can only help to reinforce the education. Always get the consent of the client first. They may have some very genuine reservations about parental involvement. You may feel that, although desirable, asking for parental involvement may risk the participation of your client in an activity and that it is better to carry on without informing the parents/carers. Your colleagues, manager and policy should support you in this.

Your organisation's policy in this area of work is essential: it should provide protection for your clients and all members of staff. If you do not have a sex and relationships policy in your organisation, talk to your manager about developing one, in partnership with parents, staff and clients.

Further information

See How **fpa** can help you and **fpa** publications and resources in the Bibliography – both at the end of this book.

See also Further information in Question 12.

Contact a Family, *Growing Up, Sex and Relationships: A Booklet to Support Parents of Young Disabled People* (Contact a Family, 2005).

14

Do I have to tell my adult client's parents/carers if I know my client is having sex?

Some parents/carers would expect staff to report any sexual activity by their son or daughter. Some staff would want to inform parents/carers as they feel that parents/carers would want to know. Many parents/carers have difficulty with the developing sexuality of their son or daughter. Parents/carers of more dependent people with severe learning disabilities may be even more protective, and extremely cautious about any sexual issues, whatever the age of their children.

Some staff have told us that parents/carers become unhappy about a developing relationship, either because they do not want their son or daughter to have any relationship, or because they disapprove of that particular partner. Staff are then asked to keep the couple from meeting, which can stop a potentially rewarding relationship.

Your duty is to your client, not to his or her parents/carers. Your client has a right to privacy and confidentiality, just like anybody else. This should be an important part of the policy of any adult service, and it is important that parents/carers know about this right, and understand it from the beginning.

It could of course be really helpful for parents/carers to know about a sexual relationship, as they could give support and understanding at an important time. You could offer your client help to tell them, or your client may give you permission to tell them. If the client does not want them to know then you cannot tell parents/carers anything about the client's private life.

If you have concerns that your client is having sex that is abusive, exploitative or risky in any way then you must consult your manager about the best way forward to protect your client.

What the law, good practice and guidance say ...

If two clients are having sex with each other you should ensure that the sex is non-abusive by ascertaining that the clients are:

- able to consent to the activity
- mutually consenting
- not exerting any element of power over one another.

If you do think it is abusive you should check your organisation's policy. Although the clients' relationship may be legal you need your organisation's policy to support you in keeping the relationship confidential. You may feel you want to provide additional support and advice to the couple, about contraception, safer sex or relationship skills. If you don't think it's abusive you will still need to check your organisation's policies.

If a client is having sex with someone who is not another client then the factors above still apply, as long as you are able to determine that the relationship is non-abusive. Your client has a right to confidentiality regarding their sexual activity and if you have no reason to be concerned that the situation is abusive then other support (for example, contraceptive advice) may be appropriate, if agreed to by your client. Your organisation's policy may suggest that you report this to your manager for your own protection, as determining non-abusiveness in a relationship could be a complex process. If this is done, and you have no additional concerns, then the extent of your responsibility in this particular situation may end.

Where a client does not currently have capacity, parents/carers have no legal rights over their actions but they may be able to influence their son's or daughter's decisions.

Where a client is proved not to have capacity, parents/carers may be involved in the decisions about their care, where this involves the client's best interests. However, this does not extend to making a decision about whether someone with a learning disability should engage in sexual activity (see Question 15).

[Mental Capacity Act 2005]

Further information

British Institute of Learning Disabilities and the West Midlands Learning Disability Forum, *Social and Personal Relationships* (British Institute of Learning Disabilities, 2001).

Drury J, Hutchinson L and Wright J, *Holding On, Letting Go* (Souvenir Press, 2000).

Outsiders, *Sex and Learning Disabilities* (Outsiders, 2006).

15

Can my clients choose their own medical treatment without involving their parents/carers?

Some people with a learning disability will have little experience of making choices, and parents/carers will naturally take on responsibility for their decisions about medical treatment. In the past, some medical practitioners used to ask for consent signatures from parents/carers of adult clients, even if it meant travelling long distances to obtain them. There was never any legal basis for this.

A client aged 16 and over with capacity to consent can make their own decisions about medical treatment without involving their parents/carers. They can change their doctor if they want to.

A client aged 15 or under can have confidential treatment as well if they can understand what is happening and it is in their best interests. All patients of any age have a right to confidentiality (see Question 17).

A client aged 17 or under cannot refuse treatment which is deemed to be in their best interests; however, a doctor would always try to get the young patient's consent if possible. In some cases the best interests of the young person may have to be decided by the court.

An adult client with capacity (18 and over) has the right to refuse any medical treatment, whatever the consequences, unless it is compulsory treatment for a mental disorder (for someone sectioned under the Mental Health Act). But this only applies if you are sure that they understand these consequences fully and are able to grasp the implications of their decision. In some cases you should go to considerable lengths to be sure the consequences are understood. For example, some decisions might have life limiting consequences, such as refusing an HIV test or a cervical screening test, or some might result in someone not receiving pain relieving drugs that another patient would be given routinely. Emergency treatment in a client's best interests could not be refused.

If clients do not have capacity, then doctors can make decisions that are in the client's best interest, and it is good practice for them to consult other people, including parents/carers, as part of their decision, usually in a best interests meeting. Where there are disagreements in best interests meetings, cases may be referred to the Court of Protection, under the Mental Capacity Act 2005.

What the law, good practice and guidance say ...

Clients aged 16 and over with a learning disability should always be helped to make their own decisions about medical treatment which will often mean additional support for them. Under 16 year olds can also make their own decisions, if medical staff feel that they understand the treatment and the consequences of it. Some under 16 year olds will need a lot of support to do this, and some will need to have the decision made for them.

The Mental Capacity Act 2005 assumes that everyone has the capacity to consent until proved otherwise (see Question 1). It sets out a framework for decision making. It allows a doctor to carry out an act in connection with care and treatment of a person, provided that it has been established that the person lacks capacity and any action is in the person's best interests. It also introduces a new legal duty to consult with parents before carrying out acts in relation to a person who lacks capacity.

In determining what may be in the person's best interests the Mental Capacity Act states that the following must be taken into account:

● whether it is likely that the person will at some time have capacity in relation to the matter in question, and

● if it appears that he will, when that is likely to be.

The person must be encouraged to participate in any decision affecting him and the following must be considered:

● the person's past and present wishes and feelings

● the beliefs and values that would be likely to influence his decision if he had capacity

● the other factors that he would be likely to consider if he were able to do so.

And, where possible, the views of the following people must be taken into account:

● anyone named by the person to be consulted in matters of this kind

● anyone engaged in caring for the person, or interested in his welfare

● anyone vested with a lasting power of attorney granted by the person, and

● any deputy appointed by the court.

[Mental Capacity Act 2005]

If there is doubt about the capacity of an individual, treatment which is urgently needed to save life may be given.

Children without capacity

Where a young person under 18 lacks capacity to consent, consent can be given on their behalf by any one person with parental responsibility or by a court of law.

This person must have the capacity to consent to the act in question, and be fully informed. The best interests of the young person must be paramount to any decision.

Even where a young person lacks capacity to consent on their own behalf, it is good practice to involve the young person as much as possible in the decision making process.

If a parent has made a decision regarding a young person under the age of 18 which you, as a care worker, teacher, social worker or other professional do not agree with, this could also be referred to the courts. A 'Section 8 Order' could be carried out, the young person made a ward of court, or the court asked to make the final decision.

[Children Act 1989]

A sterilisation decision would now always go to the Court of Protection.

CASE STUDY

Re D (a minor) (wardship: sterilisation) [1976]
Law Report: Family Division 185

An 11-year-old girl from Sheffield with Sotos Syndrome (a genetic condition causing physical overgrowth during the first years of life accompanied by delayed social development) was scheduled for a sterilisation. Her mother had been the sole parent since the girl's father died. Prior to his death, the girl's mother and father had decided that they would apply for sterilisation for the girl when she was old enough as they were worried about her getting pregnant and having a child with a disability. Their family doctor, who had been very supportive towards the family, helped the mother with this decision and said that he could arrange to sterilise the girl when she was 11 years old.

The girl's head teacher and her social worker brought this case to court when they heard that the sterilisation had been scheduled and the girl was made a ward of court. The head teacher testified to the improvement that the girl had made in the previous few years and that there was no reason to expect that the girl could not improve significantly well over the next few years so that it was feasibly possible that she may want and be able to have a child.

The court upheld this opinion and did not grant the right for the sterilisation to go ahead.

Further information

See How **fpa** can help you and **fpa** publications and resources in the Bibliography – both at the end of this book.

British Medical Association and The Law Society, *Assessment of Mental Capacity: Guidance for Doctors and Lawyers* (BMJ Books, 2004).

Department of Health, *Consent: A Guide for People with Learning Disabilities* (Department of Health, 2001).

Department of Health, *Reference Guide to Consent for Examination or Treatment* (Department of Health, 2001).

Harbour A, *Children with Mental Disorder and the Law: A Guide to Law and Practice* (Jessica Kingsley Publishers, 2008).

QUESTION

16

Can my client be given contraception, treatment or tests, such as for HIV, without their knowing what it is for?

S ometimes people are given a contraceptive method, such as the combined pill or the contraceptive injection, without being told what it is for. We have heard about contraception being given to someone who was trying to get pregnant, on the pretext that it would help a problem with her stomach. This is against the law, as the contraception must be in the person's best interests and they have to consent to it, and understand what it is for, before it can be given.

If you think that your client is being misled like this, discuss it with your manager immediately and do not help to administer the contraception as you could be taking part in an assault.

As with Question 15, if someone cannot understand the nature of the contraceptive method, doctors can decide for them, provided they consult carers and make sure it is in the client's best interests (and not for someone else's convenience). But if the client can understand, even if it might take some time to explain, then the client must make their own decision.

This is also true for male and female sterilisation, or abortion. If people can understand, they must decide for themselves (with help and support) whether or not they want the procedure.

If someone cannot understand, sterilisation can only happen after a special legal declaration is arranged. This will check that all other types of contraception have been found unsuitable and that the sterilisation is genuinely in the person's best interests. In the past a woman was sometimes given a hysterectomy to stop her periods, as it was assumed she would never be able to have children. At one time, especially in hospitals, sterilisation was used to allow sexual activity to be ignored, as pregnancy would not occur. There may have been good intentions here but it allowed sex to happen without obvious consequences and meant that abuse and sexually transmitted infections both spread unnoticed.

The law allows a woman to have an abortion up to 24 weeks of pregnancy, if two doctors agree that it is less likely to cause harm to her physical or mental health than continuing with the pregnancy.

A client would also need to give their consent to having a test or giving a sample. Someone having a test for a sexually transmitted infection should be fully aware of what a positive or negative result would mean to them and have the opportunity to discuss it beforehand. We have heard of doctors being asked to secretly test a client for HIV when consent has to be given by the client to a test of this sort.

Again, if a client is not able to consent to the test then the decision can be made for them if it is in his or her best interests.

What the law, good practice and guidance say ...

Contraception

Contraceptive methods can be divided into those with:

● **No user failure** – these do not depend on remembering to take or remembering to use contraception.

● **User failure** – these are methods people have to use and think about regularly or each time they have sex. For these methods to be effective they must be used according to the instructions.

All contraceptive methods are for women except for male condoms and male sterilisation.

There are no legal restrictions on the supply of condoms as they are not classified as treatment.

Free contraception, including emergency contraception, is available from a range of services.

All sexual health services are confidential. This means that personal information, any information about a visit and the tests and treatments that have been given will not be shared with anyone outside that service without the client's permission. However, health professionals may need to involve other services if they believe a client, or another person, to be at significant risk of harm (such as physical or sexual abuse).

If a woman does not have the capacity to consent to use a contraceptive method, a doctor could legally make a decision about her contraceptive method, and this should be in consultation with the people concerned with the woman's care. This issue is more ethical than legal, and the needs and best interests of the individual should be the focus of the decision.

Male and female sterilisation is a permanent method of contraception. If imposed upon someone, it could be said to go against Article 12 of the Human Rights Act 1998: the right to marry and have a family. The House of Lords has made it clear that sterilisation should not be used without their consent to prevent women with learning disabilities from getting pregnant.

Cases do exist where women with no capacity to consent have been ordered by the court to be sterilised.

CASE STUDY

Re A (Re A (Male Sterilisation) 2000 1 FLR 549)

The Court of Appeal ruled that a 28-year-old man with Down's syndrome could not be sterilised without his permission, which he could not give. His mother had tried to win a court order in favour of sterilisation because she believed he was sexually active and was worried that he would get someone pregnant. However, the court ruled that this reason for sterilisation was not strictly in the man's best interests, but more to protect others.

Sterilisation should not be used as an excuse to avoid taking responsibility for potential abuse and other sexual health issues. It is also important to know that sterilisation is meant to be permanent. There are reversal operations, but they are not always successful.

Abortion

In Great Britain (England, Scotland and Wales) the law (Abortion Act 1967, as amended by the Human Fertilisation and Embryology Act 1990) allows a woman to have an abortion up to 24 weeks of pregnancy, if two doctors agree that it is less likely to cause harm to her physical or mental health than continuing with the pregnancy.

Most abortions (90 out of 100) are carried out before 13 weeks of pregnancy. 98 out of 100 are carried out before 20 weeks.

An abortion can be done after 24 weeks if there are exceptional circumstances, for example if there is a serious risk to the woman's health or there is a substantial risk of physical or mental disability if the baby was born.

Other tests/treatment

Carrying out unnecessary tests and treatment on an adult who does not have the capacity to consent could be classified as an assault (a similar situation to provision of contraception).

However, if the test or treatment is in the best interests of the individual, it can be carried out. Again, every effort should be made to involve your client in the decision.

[Mental Capacity Act 2005]

Treatment and advice to under 16s

Young people under 16 accessing sexual health services have the same right to confidentiality as anyone else but health professionals may need to involve other services if they believe the young person, or another person, to be at significant risk of harm (such as physical or sexual abuse).

Young people can have an abortion without telling their parents. Health professionals should encourage them to involve parents or carers, or another supportive adult but if they choose not to do this, they can still have an abortion if the doctors believe it is in their best interests, and that they fully understand what is involved.

A health professional is justified in proceeding without the parent's consent or knowledge provided the Fraser guidelines are followed. These were a result of the case law detailed below:

Gillick v West Norfolk & Wisbech Area Health Authority [1986] AC 112

In England, in 1982, Victoria Gillick sought a High Court ruling against her local area health authority and the Department of Health and Social Security (DHSS) to prevent advice being given to her daughters without her consent. The case was dismissed, but the Appeal Court overturned this in 1984, judging parental consent to be important. An appeal to the House of Lords resulted in DHSS guidance being re-instated in 1985 and the production of guidelines, known as the Fraser Guidelines, which apply in England and Wales.

The Fraser Guidelines are based on maturity rather than age. They are:

A doctor or other professional can proceed to provide treatment or advice without the parents' knowledge or consent if it is established that:

- the young person understands the advice
- he/she can't be persuaded to inform a parent/carer
- he/she is likely to have sex anyway whether or not the treatment or advice is given
- his/her physical or mental health would suffer without the advice or treatment
- his/her best interests require it.

These guidelines exist for all young people including those with learning disabilities who have the capacity to consent to sexual activity.

It is an offence for anyone to arrange or facilitate anything that would lead to a child sex offence. This does not include offering advice or providing contraception to under 16 year olds, where these actions are within the remit of a person's job: these are the exceptions to this offence.

[Sexual Offences Act 2003]

The four circumstances where the exception applies are when someone is:

- protecting the child from sexually transmitted infections
- protecting the physical safety of the child
- preventing the child becoming pregnant
- promoting the child's emotional wellbeing by giving advice.

Further information

> See How **fpa** can help you and **fpa** publications and resources in the Bibliography – both at the end of this book.

British Medical Association, *Consent Toolkit* (British Medical Association, 2003).

Cambridge P, *HIV, Sex and Learning Disability* (Pavilion Publishing, 1997).

Cambridge P, 'The HIV testing of a man with learning disabilities: informed consent, confidentiality, and policy', *Journal of Adult Protection*, vol 3, no 4 (2001), 23–28.

Department for Children, Schools and Families, *Enabling Young People to Access Contraceptive and Sexual Health Advice – Guidance for Youth Support Workers* (Department for Children, Schools and Families, 2005).

Department for Children, Schools and Families, *Enabling Young People to Access Contraceptive and Sexual Health Advice. Legal and Policy Framework for Social Workers, Residential Social Workers, Foster Carers and other Social Care Practitioners* (Department for Children, Schools and Families, 2005).

Department of Health, *Best Practice Guidance for Doctors and Other Health Professionals on the Provision of Advice and Treatment to Young People Under 16 on Contraception, Sexual and Reproductive Health* (Department of Health, 2004).

General Medical Council, *Consent: Patients and Doctors Making Decisions Together* (General Medical Council, 2008).

McCarthy M, *Sexuality and Women with Learning Disabilities* (Jessica Kingsley Publishers, 1999).

17

Can my clients use the local sexual health clinic?

A nyone who has unprotected sex may be at risk of getting a sexually transmitted infection and may need to be tested and treated. They may also be at risk of an unplanned pregnancy and need contraceptive advice. You can get sexual health advice and information at:

- General practices (your local/family doctor).
- Specialist contraceptive clinics.
- Sexual health clinics.
- Sexually transmitted infection testing clinics (genitourinary medicine (GUM) clinics).
- Pharmacies.
- Specialist sexual assault centres.

Clinics that provide contraception and infection testing services are called sexual health clinics.

All these clinics are open to everybody, although some may have age limits, for example some services are for under 25s only. Everyone has the right to free contraception, including emergency contraception, and it is available from a range of services including contraception clinics. Most clinics also provide free condoms.

Not all clinics are experienced in helping people with learning disabilities so you may want to check this out in advance. You can find your nearest clinic by telephoning **fpa**'s helpline or using **fpa**'s online clinic finder at www.fpa.org.uk.

You may want to go along with your client on their first visit to support them. The nurses and doctors will talk with the client to assess their sexual health needs, but you may need to help if people have difficulty understanding your client.

What the law, good practice and guidance say ...

The role of a sexual health service is to provide free, confidential advice, treatment and information on sexual health, including contraception, to men and women of all ages, regardless of disability. The information should be provided by health professionals in a non-judgemental way.

The NHS Trusts and Primary Care Trusts (Sexually Transmitted Diseases) Directions 2000 says that all necessary steps should be taken to protect the identity of someone being examined or treated for a sexually transmitted infection, and the identity can only be disclosed to someone who is involved in the treatment process or preventing the spread of the infection. This legislation is usually thought of as applying just to GUM clinics but it applies wherever a sexually transmitted infection is tested for or treated. It means that all sexual health services carrying out sexually transmitted infection testing are confidential and to breach that confidentiality is against the law.

Most areas of England and Wales will have access to a sexual health clinic, although many only open once or twice a week. These may offer services for all ages, or specifically for young people. Brook runs clinics in England for under 25s.

All sexual health services are confidential. Young people under 16 accessing sexual health services have the same right to confidentiality as anyone else but health professionals may need to involve other services if they believe the young person, or another person, to be at significant risk of harm (such as physical or sexual abuse). Carers may be useful in a consultation with people with learning disabilities to help explain what is happening and to remember any advice. However, staff should check that clients are happy for their carers to be present.

Further information

See How **fpa** can help you and **fpa** publications and resources in the Bibliography – both at the end of this book.

Department for Children, Schools and Families, *Enabling Young People to Access Contraceptive and Sexual Health Advice – Guidance for Youth Support Workers* (Department for Children, Schools and Families, 2005).

Department for Children, Schools and Families, *Enabling Young People to Access Contraceptive and Sexual Health Advice. Legal and Policy Framework for Social Workers, Residential Social Workers, Foster Carers and other Social Care Practitioners* (Department for Children, Schools and Families, 2005).

What sorts of records should I keep about intimate aspects of my clients' personal lives?

People with learning disabilities have records kept of all aspects of their lives to enable proper planning and review of how their needs are met. Many people have access to these records, so it is not appropriate for intimate and personal details, for example about sexual behaviour, to be held in quite the same public way.

Sensitive information could include assessments of someone's level of sexual knowledge and awareness, made in order to plan appropriate sex and relationships education. There could also be records of whether someone's sexual behaviour has caused concern, or information about sexual health issues. All this information should not go beyond the immediate staff who need to know. It should never be a matter for gossip or jokes.

It is good practice for staff to sign up to a confidentiality policy which will make clear what information needs to be kept private and what can be shared with others.

Everyone has a right to privacy, so you need to keep records of personal information in such a way that you can justify who has access to it.

Some services keep separate records for very intimate information, and store these records with a greater level of confidentiality and security.

What the law, good practice and guidance say ...

Keeping records is important, for the support of your client, to enable a high and consistent standard of care for them, and to document your decisions and actions in relation to your client. It is especially important to record information relating to your client's sexual behaviour if you have concerns about this, as these records can help you when reporting to a manager or discussing the situation with another member of staff.

It is important to remember that anything that identifies, or refers to, a client which is written down could be part of that client's record. This could be an entry into a computer database or a scribbled note in a book.

[Data Protection Act 1998]

Any notes could be used for legal purposes so it is important to be clear in your record keeping and use as many of the client's own words as is possible.

Current legislation does not say whether or in what form records should be made.

The Data Protection Act 1998 created a new category of 'sensitive, personal data' that includes information about physical or mental health and sexual life.

This information cannot be shared with outside third parties without the explicit consent of your client. Your organisation should have guidelines stating who has access to such data within the organisation and you should know who will be able to read the client's records.

All written records should be kept securely stored in a locked area. All electronic data should have a password, making the data inaccessible to those not directly involved.

Further information

Brown H, *Making Records Work: Recording with Care in Learning Disability Services* (Pavilion Publishing and Department of Health, 2001).

Nursing and Midwifery Council, *Record Keeping: Guidance for Nurses and Midwives* (Nursing and Midwifery Council, 2009).

19

If a client tells me about a case of sexual abuse, what do I do about it?

Sometimes the procedures about sexual abuse are not clear for staff who are concerned about doing the right thing to ensure their client is protected and supported following a disclosure about abuse. If your client is under 18 then follow the child protection procedures set out by your employer or local area.

Your client has the right to go directly to the police if they want to, and you can support them to do this. Usually, however, an adult client will be asking you for help and you will follow your own employer's guidance on who to contact first and what to do next. Every member of staff needs to know where to find a copy of such guidance. If in doubt, contact a manager. If you can't get hold of anybody, and don't know what to do, contact the police and/or social services yourself.

What the law, good practice and guidance say ...

Each organisation will have its own procedures to follow about abuse. The following suggestions are some dos and don'ts that you can follow when a client tells you they have been sexually abused.

Dos

- Do accept what is being said.
- Do stay calm.
- Do listen patiently.
- Do reassure the person they are doing the right thing in telling you.
- Do explain what you are going to do:
  — if necessary, you will get emergency medical treatment for them
  — you will treat the information seriously
  — you will report it to the appropriate manager
  — you and the manager will take steps to protect the individual.

- Do report to the appropriate manager as soon as you can. In most circumstances, it is likely that a decision to call the police would rest with the manager, not the client's care worker. However, in an emergency and when a manager cannot be contacted, you should inform the police if you suspect that a crime (for example, a sexual assault or rape) has taken place.

- Do write a factual account of the conversation you had with the individual as soon as you can. Try as far as possible to write down the person's own words. This may also be used as part of a legal action.

Don'ts

- Don't appear shocked, horrified, disgusted or angry.

- Don't press the individual for details (it is not your job to launch into an investigation).

- Don't contaminate or remove possible forensic evidence. If the reported incident happened very recently it may still be possible for the police to obtain forensic evidence. Do not give the person a wash or bath, or food and drink until after the medical examination.

- Don't promise to keep secrets – you have a duty to pass on information to the appropriate person.

- Don't give sweeping reassurances such as "Now you have told someone this will never happen to you again" – no one can give such a guarantee.

- Don't confront the alleged abuser.

Adapted from: Image in Action,
Yarrow's Guidelines on Dealing with Suspected Abuse (Yarrow Housing Ltd, 2002).

Further information

Department of Health and Home Office, *No Secrets: Guidance on Developing and Implementing Multi-agency Policies and Procedures to Protect Vulnerable Adults from Abuse* (Department of Health and Home Office Communications Directorate, 2000).

Consent
Consent offers a range of services to people with learning disabilities, including enabling informed choices, sexual health, issues of HIV risks and working with people with learning disabilities who have been sexually abused or perpetrated sexual abuse.
Tel: 01923 670796
www.hertsparts.nhs.uk

Respond (see Question 3).

Voice UK (see Question 3).

WITNESS
WITNESS is a charity which aims to promote safe boundaries between professionals and the public in order to prevent abuse.
Helpline: 0845 4500 300
www.popan.org.uk

Am I allowed to help clients who need support to get hold of pornography?

Many staff are sympathetic to the sexual needs and desires of their adult clients and respect their right to look at the same kinds of magazines, videos, DVDs, books and internet images as everyone else. Some staff want to know where they stand with helping clients (aged 18 and over) get hold of these materials.

All types of staff can sometimes be offended by pornographic images on people's bedroom walls. Some clients are forbidden from having any posters and pictures at all.

Some pornography is legal, but some pornography, for example showing indecent or abusive images of children, is not. The difference between them is not clear cut, but as a general rule you can rely on anything for sale in a major high street newsagent as being legal. Any indecent or abusive images of children are against the law.

A client has a right to buy magazines or videos available legally to anybody else. If shopping help is needed, and you do not approve of pornography, then it would be fair to get someone else to buy them instead. Your employer may cover this in a policy or guidelines.

You may have to come to some compromise over the posters issue, as staff have the right not to be exposed to offensive materials in the course of their work. Perhaps pictures could go inside a cupboard door, or be covered up when cleaners and other staff come in. The room does belong to that client and staff have no right to remove or destroy clients' property because they disapprove of it. Clients should be helped to understand that pornography should be kept and used in private.

If you find pornography that may not be legal in a client's possession then you do not have to do anything about it unless it involves or appears to involve children. You must report any indecent or abusive images of children to the police in order to help protect the children involved.

Some images downloaded from the internet can be more extreme than images in pornographic magazines. All extreme pornography is illegal, and clients (or anyone else) could be prosecuted for having looked at these images on a computer. If the images include children, you have an obligation to report them to the police as they can help protect the children in the images by tracking down the perpetrators.

Sometimes legal images of children can be collected and used in an illegal way (for example, pictures of naked children collected from parenting magazines). If in doubt, you should seek advice.

It is illegal for staff to show pornography to a client for the purpose of sexually exciting the staff member. If you are using explicit material in a sex and relationships education (SRE) lesson, make sure that your lesson is properly planned and recorded so that you are not open to such accusations.

Guidance would be different for people with learning disabilities in secure NHS provision. Following the Ashworth Inquiry[7] secure services all have a very restrictive policy on pornography.

What the law, good practice and guidance say ...

Buying and owning pornography showing adults (except extreme pornography) is legal as long as you are an adult (aged 18 or over). Any person shown in this pornography must be aged 18 and over. This provision was introduced in 2003; the legal age was previously 16 and over.

[Sexual Offences Act 2003]

It is legal to physically help a client to buy legal pornography, just as it would be if you helped them go to any shop or reach any magazine or video which is for sale to the public. In addition, providing satellite television in a client's private bedroom which would enable them to choose to watch pornographic films is legal.

Legally, where staff stand with internet access is much more difficult to state clearly, as helping a client to access legal internet pornography sites could very easily lead the client to illegal sites and images. However, clients have a right to be taught to use the internet, just like anyone else. Some organisations have restricted access to the internet so that pornographic sites cannot be accessed.

Owning pornography showing indecent or abusive images of children (aged 17 and under) is illegal in any form. Legislation relating to images of children is included in the Protection of Children Act 1978, the Sexual Offences Act 2003 and the Criminal Justice Act 1988.

---

[7] Fallon P et al, *Report on the Committee of Inquiry into the Personality Disorder Unit, Ashworth Special Hospital* (The Stationery Office, 1999).

These acts make it illegal to:

- take or make any indecent photograph of a child
- distribute or show such photographs
- own these photographs with a view to them being shown or distributed
- publish anything advertising the distribution of these images.

This provision also applies to images downloaded from the internet as computer generated images are classified as photographs.

[Criminal Justice and Public Order Act 1994]

Owning pornography of adults who look like children is illegal. This would apply when a 'reasonable person' would say that the people involved in the pornographic images look under 18, even when they are actually adults.

[Criminal Justice and Public Order Act 1994]

Owning pornography showing extreme violent images became illegal in 2008. According to the Criminal Justice and Immigration Act 2008, images that include necrophilia (sex with corpses), bestiality (sex with animals) or violence that is life threatening or likely to result in serious injury to the anus, breasts or genitals, are now illegal to possess for personal use.

Although the use of pornography in SRE with adults with learning disabilities is something which can cause controversy within organisations, the use of explicit material for SRE purposes is not illegal. The reasons for using explicit images rather than more abstract ones should be recorded and explained, and will usually be because the person being educated cannot relate to abstract images and will not learn from them. If someone is showing people with learning disabilities sexual images for their own sexual gratification then this is illegal (see Question 9).

A client I am working with has expressed a wish to pay for a prostitute. Am I allowed to support him/her in this?

Some clients will never be able to form relationships for themselves yet have sexual feelings and frustrations like anybody else. Prostitutes (sometimes called sex workers) offer sex for money and either staff or the clients themselves may ask about whether it is legal for clients to use the services of a prostitute. Some agencies in Europe specialise in offering paid sex services to people with disabilities.

It is not against the law to be, or to use a prostitute if the prostitute is 18 or over. There is nothing to stop your client, who has capacity to consent, visiting or being visited by a prostitute (if they live somewhere without regulations about this), as long as it is your client who is making the arrangement and not you. It is illegal to control or gain from prostitution so, if you support a client with this, be particularly careful to make sure that you are not negotiating or dealing with the money side of things.

Part of your duty of care to your client might be to advise on safer sex and to make sure that they understand the role of a prostitute and that buying sex is different to being in a relationship with someone. You might also make sure that he or she is not being systematically exploited over money.

You may have guidance from your employer on this issue, which either supports or forbids carers from assisting clients to use the services of prostitutes. There may well be house rules in shared residential accommodation about whether visitors are permitted in bedrooms.

What the law, good practice and guidance say ...

A 'prostitute' is defined as a person (male or female) who, at least once, offers or provides sexual services to another person in return for payment or a promise of payment.

[Sexual Offences Act 2003]

It is a common belief that prostitution is illegal. Having sex for money and paying for sex are not illegal but there are currently more than 35 provisions relating to prostitution which are. Someone who pays for sex would be committing a crime if the sex was with someone under-age, non-consenting or a victim of trafficking. Terms such as 'soliciting' and 'kerb crawling' are used to describe some of the illegal aspects of the trade.

Anyone wishing to pay a prostitute for sex must stay within the law, which means not kerb crawling or outraging public decency. This also applies to people with learning disabilities. An additional concern is the capacity to consent of your client, who must be able to agree to the activity, or it would be illegal.

Since 2003 it has been illegal to pay (or have another financial arrangement) for otherwise legal sex with anyone aged 17 or under. The control of a prostitute aged under 18 is a very serious offence with a penalty of up to 14 years in prison. Your client would need to be aware of the age of any prostitute they paid for sex.

[Sexual Offences Act 2003]

Anybody, male or female, selling sex on the street could be found guilty of solicitation.

During 2009, the Government proposed changes to the law on paying for sex, which was under review at the time this edition was published.

Further information

Outsiders, *Disabled People and Paid Sex* (Outsiders, 2006).

International Union of Sex Workers
Offers free and confidential advice, information and support and has a good legal section on its website.
Tel: 07946 897770
www.iusw.org

Outsiders
Outsiders is a nationwide, self-help community providing mailings and events where people meet up and practise socialising. Many of its projects address sexual surrogacy and sexual expression for people with disabilities. Although not specifically aimed at people with learning disabilities, it provides a social service for people with physical and social disabilities.
Tel: 020 7354 8291
Sex and disability helpline: 0707 499 3527
www.outsiders.org.uk

www.sw5.info/law.htm
A site for male and transgender sex workers with information on UK law.

22

I think my client is gay: is the law different for them?

The law used to be very different for lesbian, gay and bisexual people but most of the differences have been removed.

The age of consent is now the same for everybody (16 years old). Gay or lesbian couples cannot get married, but they can declare a civil partnership.

If your client is lesbian, gay or bisexual, then an issue for him or her may be accepting that themselves. Finding acceptance from others, such as staff and parents/carers, and avoiding discrimination, will also be very important to your client. Moving away from the assumption that all clients are heterosexual is a necessary process for organisations. It is now illegal to discriminate against or insult someone at work on the grounds of their sexual orientation, and all health and social care employers should have a policy that prevents staff from discriminating in this way.

It is perfectly legal to support your client in understanding his or her sexual identity and feeling positive about it. This can include giving information about support lines and where to meet other lesbian, gay or bisexual people socially. As with any referral, you may want to check out a support line to make sure that it is genuine and not set up to exploit vulnerable callers.

What the law, good practice and guidance say ...

If a person with learning disabilities thinks they may be lesbian, gay or bisexual they should be offered full support by workers to help them explore their sexuality. This could perhaps involve contacting agencies to meet other lesbian, gay or bisexual people, or to access specific support or counselling.

Direct and indirect discrimination and harassment of homosexual people in the workplace is illegal. All benefits offered to heterosexual employees should automatically be offered to homosexual employees.

[Employment Equality (Sexual Orientation) Regulations 2003]

Prior to the Sexual Offences Act 2003 there were a number of offences which covered (directly or otherwise) sex between men: for example, buggery, gross indecency, solicitation by men for immoral purposes and procuring others to commit homosexual acts. Female homosexuality was largely unmentioned directly in law.

These offences were either repealed, or made gender neutral by the 2003 Sexual Offences Act.

It is now legal for more than two men to take part in a sexual act, in private, as long as they are all consenting and have capacity to consent.

The repeal of Section 28

Section 28 was the common name for Section 2a of the Local Government Act 1986. It was repealed on 10 July 2003 in the House of Lords. This Section prohibited local authorities in England and Wales from promoting homosexuality.

Section 28 did not apply to schools but nonetheless it had a significant impact on many schools because teachers wrongly thought it restricted them from discussing homosexuality in the classroom.

Further information

Abbot D and Howarth J, *Secret Loves, Hidden Lives? Exploring Issues for Men and Women with Learning Difficulties who are Gay, Lesbian or Bisexual* (The Policy Press, 2005).

Cambridge P, *HIV, Sex and Learning Disability* (Pavilion Publishing, 1997).

FFLAG
Dedicated to supporting parents and their gay, lesbian and bisexual sons and daughters.
Helpline: 0845 652 0311
www.fflag.org.uk

Get Connected
Puts vulnerable young people in touch with appropriate services.
Helpline: 0808 808 4994
www.getconnected.org.uk

LGBT Network Cymru, The
Information, advice and feedback for lesbian, gay and bisexual communities, their families and friends in South Wales.
Tel: 01792 645325
www.geocities.com/swansea_bay_lgb

London Lesbian and Gay Switchboard
Information and support, and social and specialist services for lesbian, gay and bisexual people.
Helpline: 020 7837 7324
www.llgs.org.uk

Pink Parents
A range of support services and social activities for all lesbian, gay, bisexual and transgender families.
Helpline: 08701 273 274
www.pinkparents.org.uk

Sappho Service, The
Offers clinical and counselling services to lesbians, bisexual women and women who have sex with women.
Tel: 0141 211 8130
www.sandyford.org

Stonewall
Stonewall lobbies for equality for lesbian, gay and bisexual people on the mainstream political agenda. It promotes new research and takes test legal cases that challenge inequality.
Tel: 020 7593 1850
www.stonewall.org.uk

Is it legal to touch my client's private parts in order to wash them or give healthcare or treatment?

S ome people have a range of health needs that include being unable to go to the toilet by themselves or to keep themselves clean without help, and they may also need other kinds of intimate care. When people can make a choice you must ask their permission before providing any physical care. If they cannot decide for themselves you still have a duty to provide the care they need.

If someone cannot give consent, you could be at risk of being accused of sexual assault, so be sure that when you give care there is no way that anyone could think that what you are doing is sexual. As long as a reasonable person would agree that you are providing care and not being abusive you are protected.

Sometimes it comes as a shock to new staff to have to provide intimate care, as it breaks the usual social rules about privacy and seeing other people's naked bodies. This can occasionally lead to staff stepping over the line between care acts and sexual acts, as they may feel that as one set of rules has already been broken others can be too. Your organisation should give you appropriate training but if you are not sure about what you are doing, get advice.

What the law, good practice and guidance say ...

Sexual touching without consent is illegal and could be covered either under the offences of Sexual assault [Sexual Offences Act 2003 Section 3] or Sexual activity with a person with a mental disorder impeding choice [Sexual Offences Act 2003 Section 30].

For both of these offences, a reasonable person would have to say that the touch was sexual: therefore intimate care in the course of everyday duties is not affected.

The Mental Capacity Act 2005 is very clear that the administration of certain acts in connection with the care and treatment of someone without capacity which is in their best interests is legal and is a statutory defence against liability.

The following section is taken from the Pan-Lothian Working Group's 'Making choices, keeping safe' policy with kind permission from NHS Lothian.

The dignity of people with learning disabilities must be upheld by workers at all times. Considerations should include:

- closing toilet/bathroom/bedroom doors
- consulting people with learning disabilities about their intimate care
- sensitivity: for example, being aware of appropriate use of language when talking to people with learning disabilities
- awareness of religious and cultural beliefs and practices
- the right for people with learning disabilities to choose who assists them when they need help or support with their personal care where practicable, while respecting the rights of both parties.

[Pan-Lothian Working Group]

Workers should avoid negative comments and disapproval expressed through words or body language.

Good care planning which reflects individual need and which is regularly revisited is an essential tool in managing intimate care. This can be an additional safeguard to protect clients and staff.

Intimate care should ideally be undertaken by workers that the client is familiar with and trusts. This has implications for managers in recruiting workers and forward planning of rotas. There is also the additional issue of gender and same sex care which should be considered by managers when recruiting and planning.

Sometimes a client can become sexually aroused when intimate care is being carried out. This may be because it is one of the only times that their body is touched intimately. This should be recorded and where possible, a plan put into place which creates private time for that individual and provides education about masturbation and touching the body (see Question 24).

Further information

Cambridge P and Carnaby S, 'A personal touch: managing the risks of abuse during intimate and personal care for people with learning disabilities', *Journal of Adult Protection*, vol 2, no 4 (2000), 4–16.

Cambridge P and Carnaby S, *Making it Personal: Providing Intimate and Personal Care for People with Learning Disabilities* (Pavilion Publishing, 2000).

www.mcks.scot.nhs.uk
Pan Lothian Working Group's policy website. This is an excellent policy with good, detailed guidelines.

My client is very frustrated because they cannot masturbate properly. Is it okay to teach them how to do this?

Sexual frustration may be a cause of violent and self-injuring behaviour. Some clients have never learned successful masturbation, which could relieve this frustration. There have been very good results from education programmes to teach masturbation in these circumstances. Most teaching is by pictures, discussion or signing and does not involve touching. It is legal to teach in this way but make sure you only do this as part of an organised and planned educational programme that has been agreed to meet identified needs.

There is a small group of people within society who are unable to learn skills in any way other than touch. They sometimes have multi-sensory impairments and cannot hear or see, and they sometimes have a profound learning disability. These clients may need physical prompts. This activity is against the law as it is illegal to sexually touch a client with a learning disability.

To enable this to happen you would need to have a very clear consensus from all the professionals involved that this was the only way forward and a Court of Protection decision based on a formal case conference that stated that this was in the client's best interests.

For any kind of teaching you must be able to clearly prove that it is part of a planned educational programme, and that it is not abusing or exploiting the client or giving sexual excitement to the member of staff. You must keep full records of the meetings where the programme was planned and decided, lesson plans for the teaching sessions and review notes afterwards.

No one can be compelled to do this work.

What the law, good practice and guidance say ...

If there is no touch involved in teaching masturbation there is less likely to be any legal issue, but ensure all actions are documented and supported by your organisation. Any explicit materials used will be covered by the exemption in the Sexual Offences Act 2003 where they are for the purposes of sex and relationships education (see Question 20).

Should touch be essential there are lots of considerations as this is illegal.

[Sexual Offences Act 2003]

Touching a man's or woman's genitals could be interpreted by a reasonable person as sexual touching which would be illegal under the following offences:

Sexual activity with a person with a mental disorder impeding choice

[Sexual Offences Act 2003 Section 30]

Care workers: sexual activity with a person with a mental disorder

[Sexual Offences Act 2003 Section 38]

In both of these offences, sexual activity includes any form of sexual touching.

Should touching (or assisted masturbation) be deemed essential (because an individual was injuring themselves masturbating ineffectively, for example), the court would have to make the decision that this should be carried out based on a formal case conference. It would have to be established that the activity cannot be explained to the client in question without using a hands-on method, that that method is identified by a multi-disciplinary care group as the right step to take at that particular time, and that the group identifies the person to do it and how it is to be done. The court would then have to agree the action for it to proceed.

Teaching masturbation has been used in the past as the excuse for sexual abuse, and in one particular case a head teacher took a female pupil to a hotel to enable him to 'teach' her in private. He was found guilty of sexual offences.

[R v Hall [1988] 86 Criminal Appeals Reports 159]

Organisations working in this area are divided on the issue of touch, or 'assisted masturbation'. It is essential that anyone embarking on a scheme of work relating to masturbation has the full support of other staff, and documents all actions and outcomes (see Question 18).

Clients who are masturbating ineffectively, or with objects not made specifically for that purpose might benefit from the use of a sex aid such as lubricant, a vibrator or a dildo. There are also aids specifically for people with physical impairments and or learning disabilities. Many websites sell a range of sex aids that may be suitable.

It is legal to support someone with purchasing a sex aid when the policy of your organisation supports you to do so. Clients should make their own choices and be aware of hygiene and privacy issues. If clients need help to be taught how to use a sex aid, as with any form of teaching around masturbation, models and diagrams can be used, but no contact made with your client's genitals.

Further information

See How **fpa** can help you and **fpa** publications and resources in the Bibliography – both at the end of this book.

Cambridge P, Carnaby S and McCarthy M, 'Responding to masturbation in supporting sexuality and challenging behaviour in services for people with learning disabilities', *Journal of Learning Disabilities*, vol 7, no 3 (2003), 251–266.

Hingsburger D, *Hand Made Love: A Guide for Teaching about Male Masturbation* (Diverse City Press, 1995).

Hingsburger D and Haar S, *Finger Tips: A Guide for Teaching about Female Masturbation* (Diverse City Press, 2003).

Hingsburger D and Harber M, *The Ethics of Touch: Establishing and Maintaining Appropriate Boundaries in Service to People with Developmental Disabilities* (Diverse City Press, 1998).

I know my clients are allowed to get married or live together but can I stop the marriage of a client if I think it is not a good idea?

Many myths exist about who must give permission before someone with a learning disability gets married, including whether they are allowed to at all.

Someone with a learning disability may marry someone of the opposite sex from the age of 18, or from the age of 16 if their parents/carers agree, just like anybody else in England and Wales. They may also enter into civil partnerships with someone of the same sex. The registrar or official who marries them must be satisfied that they both understand what they are doing. Occasionally the registrar may get an opinion from a doctor or other professional to help him or her decide that.

It is possible to prevent a marriage taking place, but there must be very good reasons – such as financial, emotional or physical abuse – but it is very unusual for this to happen.

Sometimes clients get married just to have their relationship taken more seriously, and sometimes in order to be given shared accommodation. We have heard some very unusual reasons given for leaving members of a couple in single accommodation, the strangest being that "building regulations forbid the construction of double rooms in a hostel". Needless to say this was and is not true! The BMA and The Law Society have produced some guidelines around capacity to consent to marriage.[8]

In some communities in England and Wales people are made to get married without their consent. Some of the time they are taken by force, without their agreement, to another country to do this. This is called forced marriage and is against the law.

What the law, good practice and guidance say ...

Article 12 of the European Convention on Human Rights incorporated into UK law by the Human Rights Act 1998 states that it is a basic human right to marry and

---

[8] British Medical Association and The Law Society, *Assessment of Mental Capacity: Guidance for Doctors and Lawyers* (BMJ Books, 2004).

have a family. A person with learning disabilities may marry someone of the opposite sex, without parental support, at 18 years of age, as anyone can.

A couple of the same sex may now have a civil union and become partners in the eyes of the law.

[Civil Partnerships Act 2004]

If the registrar doubts the capacity of a person they may ask a professional person to provide a statement to confirm their capacity.

If someone wanted to stop a marriage, they would need a very good reason and proof of their claim. Someone can enter into a caveat with the registrar which means the registrar would have to investigate the matter further. Anyone can start this procedure, but if the objection is deemed to be frivolous, they could be liable to pay costs and damages. Where the couple marry in church, the objection would be to the banns.

[Marriage Act 1949 Section 29]

Clients are legally allowed to live together, like anyone else. The issues surrounding this are often practical, such as who will fund the accommodation, if they are from different counties, and how much support they will need. Living together or marriage will mean that the person's financial and legal obligations will change. Workers may need to help the person with learning disabilities to access appropriate information and advice.

The law recognises that a mental disorder may make someone unfit for marriage, but for this to be used to contest the validity of the marriage it would need to be proved that there was no awareness of the disability at the time of marriage.

Divorce

The law relating to divorce treats people with learning disabilities the same as everyone else. Couples who separate may need additional support, including seeking help from housing agencies and solicitors, as well as emotional support. Couples who live in residential care homes may need additional practical provision such as new accommodation provided for one of them.

Forced marriage

Forced marriage is an issue within some communities in England and Wales. The marriages themselves are often carried out abroad. These types of marriages (which are marriages without consent, with some form of duress, and not to be confused with arranged marriages which are with the consent of both parties) can often involve the abduction of a woman and can lead to her abuse, sexual assault and rape within the marriage. Any marriage without the consent of both parties is against the law. Men can also be forced into marriage.

[Matrimonial Causes Act 1973]

If you are concerned that someone is, or is going to be, forced into marriage you can help them. The Forced Marriage Civil Protection Act 2007 provides protection orders for people who have been forced into marriage or are at risk of being forced into marriage. You can make this application on behalf of your client; they do not have to do it themselves. This is a piece of civil legislation, not criminal, so it will not prosecute anyone involved in the forced marriage, it will just protect the victim. This may be important to your client if the person arranging the marriage is a family member.

Further information

British Medical Association and The Law Society, *Assessment of Mental Capacity: Guidance for Doctors and Lawyers* (BMJ Books, 2004).

Forced Marriage (Civil Protection) Act 2007
Available to download at www.opsi.gov.uk.

Home Office, *A Choice by Right* (Home Office Communications Directorate, 2000).

Forced Marriage Unit
In the UK the Forced Marriage Unit assists victims of forced marriage, and professionals working in the social, educational and health sectors who may encounter it.
Tel: 020 7008 0151
www.fco.gov.uk

Karma Nirvana
Provides support for, and campaigns on behalf of, victims and survivors of forced marriage.
Honour Network Helpline: 0800 599 9247
www.karmanirvana.org.uk

26

If a client of mine became pregnant or fathered a child, would they be allowed to keep the baby?

Some people with learning disabilities become parents and successfully bring up children with varying degrees of support required. Not everyone is comfortable with this because of concerns about the safety and development of the child. Looking after children may be beyond the capacity of some people (with or without a disability) and the support needed to enable this may not be available.

Everyone has the right to marry and have a family, but children have to be protected too. If your client has a baby or fathers a child, and it is not safe for them to bring up the child, then another home would have to be found for the child, probably with adoptive parents/carers.

What the law, good practice and guidance say …

Article 12 of the Human Rights Act states that it is everyone's right to marry and have a family.

Legally, there is nothing to stop a woman with learning disabilities who has capacity from having a child, yet the reality is often different – some women are made to have an abortion or have their children taken into care. There is nothing to stop a man with a learning disability from fathering a child but the law may prevent him from bringing up the child.

In cases where a woman who does not have the capacity to consent becomes pregnant, professionals may decide that it would be in her best interests to have an abortion. This decision would often focus on the potential harm to the mental health of the pregnant woman by carrying the baby to full term and giving birth.

There are parenting assessment packs available which deal with assessing the capability of people with learning disabilities to have and look after a child. These are sometimes criticised for being too thorough and asking people with learning disabilities to prove things that other parents do not need to. However, these may help in the assessment of a client who wishes to become a parent either before or after a pregnancy.

It is good practice, if child care proceedings threaten to remove a child from a parent with learning disabilities, to ensure the parent has an opportunity to learn parenting skills, for example in a mother and baby unit where the carers understand learning disabilities. It is also important to ensure that the person with a learning disability has a social worker of their own. The child's social worker may not understand that people with learning disabilities can act as parents.

Further information

See How **fpa** can help you and **fpa** publications and resources in the Bibliography — both at the end of this book.

Affleck F, *You and Your Baby 0–1 Years* (Change, 2004).

McGaw S, *Parent Assessment Manual 2.0* (Pill Creek Publishing, 2007).

McGaw S, *What Works for Parents with Learning Disabilities?* (Barnardo's, 2000).

Morris J, *The Right Support: Report on the Task Force on Supporting Disabled Adults in their Parenting Role* (Joseph Rowntree Foundation, 2003).

Change
A national organisation, led by disabled people, that campaigns for equal rights for people with learning disabilities.
Tel: 0113 243 0202 (Mincom: 0113 243 2225)
www.changepeople.co.uk

27

Will my client get into trouble if they expose themselves in public?

Sometimes people with learning disabilities expose their genitals in public deliberately or accidentally. This can be offensive for members of the public and for any staff who might be with them at the time.

We have heard of cases of male clients forgetting to zip up their trousers when using a public toilet, or female clients who are disturbed by their periods and remove their underwear in public when they are menstruating.

If it is clearly accidental then there is no problem; they have not done anything illegal. However, if they do it deliberately, wanting someone to see them and be alarmed and upset by it, that is against the law.

This only applies to men or women showing their genitals: bottoms and breasts are not included.

What the law, good practice and guidance say ...

The offence of Exposure *[Sexual Offences Act 2003]* replaced the previous Indecent exposure *[Vagrancy Act 1824, Town and Police Clauses Act 1847]*.

A man or woman can commit this offence if they intentionally expose their genitals intending that someone will see them and be caused alarm or distress.

No one actually has to see them: for example, they could be caught on CCTV, but they do need to intend that someone might see them.

The offence does not include naturists (who intentionally expose their genitals with no intent to cause alarm or distress to anyone). Similarly an exhibitionist streaker at a sports occasion would not be breaking this law (but risks breaking public nuisance laws).

If someone with a learning disability (usually a man) does deliberately expose himself intending to cause offence, he may be prosecuted. It is important to support him to seek appropriate treatment (for example, with a men's group).

QUESTION

28

How much trouble would my client be in if they had sex in public?

People who do not have their own home (for example, teenagers and people being cared for by others) are more likely to have sex in public places, since they may not have an appropriate private place to go to. This leaves them vulnerable to attack or abuse and they may get into trouble if they are found.

It is against the law to have sex in a public place, for example in a park or the countryside, if there is a good chance of being seen. However, if no one can see you it is not against the law. There is a different rule for sex in a public toilet, which is always against the law. This applies to toilets in pubs, restaurants and anywhere the public could go, even if inside a locked cubicle.

What the law, good practice and guidance say ...

Sexual activity in a public place is only illegal if you are somewhere you can easily be seen.

[Sexual Offences Act 2003]

Sexual activity in a public lavatory is an offence. A person commits the offence if they are in a public lavatory where the public can go (even if the door of a cubicle is locked) and they intentionally engage in sexual activity.

This is an offence that can be committed by men or women, so a heterosexual couple having sex in a night-club toilet could be liable, as could 'cottaging' – men having sex with men in public toilets.

[Sexual Offences Act 2003]

QUESTION

If my client committed a sexual offence, would they be treated the same as other people?

People with learning disabilities may commit a sexual offence, especially if they have had little or no education about appropriate sexual behaviour. Sometimes this is not taken as seriously (or is not considered a crime) as it would have been if it had been committed by a non-disabled person and staff wrongly think that if the case went to court it would be automatically dismissed. If the crime is investigated and prosecuted many people are unsure how the person would be dealt with, and whether their disability would be considered when looking at the case. This can, in some instances, lead to the client not being reported for a crime they have committed.

If a person with a learning disability has committed an offence, they should be treated in the same way as everyone else, but depending on the severity of their disability they may be directed through the forensic mental health services (a service which supports offenders with mental health problems). They have the right to put their point of view across but sometimes people with a disability need additional support with this, which should be provided for them. If the person is under 18 a different approach would be taken, as with any young person who has committed an offence.

If you know a client has committed a sexual offence speak to your line manager. If the situation is urgent and your line manager is not available, you may decide to talk directly to the police, mentioning your client's disability.

The police and legal system might decide that it would not be in anyone's interests to prosecute, and that therapy or education would be more appropriate.

What the law, good practice and guidance say ...

There is nothing in law which says that a person with a learning disability who has committed an offence will be treated any differently to anyone else.

However, it is expected that in cases where the defendant has a learning disability, this will be presented as evidence. This may include the lawyer saying that because of their disability the defendant did not understand the difference between right and wrong and had no real intention (*mens rea* – guilty state of mind) to commit the act. Or it may be that the offence was caused largely due to the defendant's disability.

The reaction of staff should not be any different if their client is the one carrying out the offence or is a victim of it. It is not the role of the staff, or the organisation, to decide whether prosecuting would be in the best interests of all involved. This is a matter for the police and the Crown Prosecution Service to decide. Regardless of any concerns over the outcome of informing the police, staff must always do so if an offence has been committed.

CASE STUDY

A young woman with learning disabilities accused a young man who was previously known to her of rape. He also had a learning disability. She told her social worker about the situation but the social worker decided that as they both had a learning disability it was unlikely that anything would be done about it and so decided that it was in both of their best interests not to take it any further.

It became known to the young woman's family that this had happened and they took it upon themselves to physically assault the young man for his alleged actions.

The case was then taken to the police following the assault who then investigated the offence of rape against the woman, and the assault against the man, and provided some form of protection for the young man and his family.

Had the social worker reported this case to the police initially the outcome could have been much less complicated.

Further information

Brown H and Thompson D, 'Service responses to men with intellectual disabilities who have unacceptable or abusive sexual behaviours: the case against inaction', *Journal of Applied Research in Intellectual Disabilities*, vol 10, no 2 (1997), 176–197.

Murphy G, Intellectual disabilities, sexual abuse and sexual offending, in Carr A et al, *Handbook of Intellectual Disability and Clinical Psychology Practice* (Routledge, 2007).

Voice UK (see Question 3).

QUESTION

30

If my client's behaviour is inappropriate (in a sexual way), do I have any responsibility for the behaviour?

You and the service you work for have two responsibilities under your duty of care to your client (see Question 5):

1 To respond to the behaviour when it happens to keep everyone safe and help your client avoid public shame, while at the same time giving a clear message that the behaviour is not acceptable. Some clients may still choose to continue the behaviour and you will have to decide what to do depending on how much harm or trouble they are causing to others and to themselves; and

2 To do what you can do to prevent future behaviour that could harm someone else or get your client into trouble or danger.

Sexually harmful behaviour can be prevented by the following:

● Protecting your client from physical or sexual abuse or violent situations especially at a young age. School toilets are one of the risk areas outside the home.

● Providing good sex and relationships education (SRE), including education about social rules such as how to greet people, about relationships and about public and private behaviour and places.

● Giving people the chance to have as much of a social life as possible.

● Being clear and consistent about what behaviour is acceptable and what is not acceptable (including what the law says) and what may upset or hurt other people.

● Making sure that supportive people around your client (including family and even friendly neighbours) know to reinforce the rules and to be watchful if any risks are known about.

All of these should be started very early in life and be kept going as long as is needed. The responsibility is not yours alone, but is shared by everyone in all the services that support your client, along with family members. Services should plan to meet these needs and understand how they help to stop sexually harmful behaviour from happening.

What the law, good practice and guidance say …

Your organisation's policy and guidelines should support you in this. They may include examples of sexually inappropriate behaviour in your clients which you can be vigilant about. They should promote good quality SRE and support for your clients. A good policy to read if your organisation does not have one is *Making choices, keeping safe* (see Further information at the end of this section).

Sometimes you have to decide whether the behaviour of a client is harmful enough to warrant intervention. A useful starting point can be found in *Who decides?* by the Law Commission. This suggests that:

> " *'Harm' should be taken to include not only ill treatment (including sexual abuse and forms of ill treatment which are not physical), but also the impairment of, or an unavoidable deterioration in, physical or mental health; and the impairment of physical, intellectual, emotional, social or behavioural development."* [9]

The issue of responsibility in this area is one which should be discussed and acted upon by your organisation as a whole as the organisation could ultimately be liable for failure of its duty of care.

Further information

Department of Health and Home Office, *No Secrets: Guidance on Developing and Implementing Multi-agency Policies and Procedures to Protect Vulnerable Adults from Abuse* (Department of Health and Home Office Communications Directorate, 2000).

Fyson R, *Young People with Learning Disabilities who Show Sexually Inappropriate or Abusive Behaviours* (Ann Craft Trust, 2005).

Lord Chancellor's Department, *Who Decides? Making Decisions on Behalf of Mentally Incapacitated Adults* (Her Majesty's Stationery Office, 1997).

Lovell E, *Children and Young People who Display Sexually Harmful Behaviour* (NSPCC Information Briefings, 2002).

Lovell E, *"I think I might need some more help with this problem": Responding to Children and Young People who Display Sexually Harmful Behaviour* (NSPCC, 2002).

---

[9] Lord Chancellor's Department, *Who Decides? Making Decisions on Behalf of Mentally Incapacitated Adults* (Her Majesty's Stationery Office, 1997).

NHS Edinburgh and Lothian, *Making Choices, Keeping Safe: Policy and Practice Guidelines on Relationships and Sexual Wellbeing when Working with People with Learning Disabilities* (NHS Edinburgh and Lothian, 2004).

Thompson D and Brown H, *Response-ability: Working with Men with Learning Disabilities who have Abusive or Unacceptable Behaviour* (Mental Health Foundation, 1999).

Stop it now! (see Question 11).

QUESTION

31

If my client is a victim of a sex crime can they give evidence in court?

A ny criminal investigation needs sufficient evidence before a prosecution can be brought. If the only evidence is the word of someone with a learning disability it may be more difficult to prosecute successfully. In the past this has prevented cases from being brought to court.

This is changing, thanks to new laws which will support people with learning disabilities, and other vulnerable witnesses, to give evidence in court. As long as someone is competent to understand and to take the oath they can give evidence. In some cases, people with learning disabilities may be able to give evidence outside of the court situation.

A number of measures can be used to make it easier in court, such as putting up a screen, so the witness does not have to see the defendant, pre-recorded interviews being used to reduce the stress on the witness, and informal clothing being worn in the court.

Vulnerable witnesses will also have access to an intermediary who is a person who will communicate with them during police interviews and throughout the trial. The intermediary will ask the witness the questions from the lawyers and provide the court with the answers from the witness. This will be especially beneficial in cases where the witness has few verbal skills.

What the law, good practice and guidance say ...

A person with a learning disability who is a victim of an offence would be assessed to determine their competency. The following things need to be established: if the witness suffers from a mental disorder, what the degree of mental disorder is and whether they can understand the oath they will take.

[Youth Justice and Criminal Evidence Act 1999]

The following changes to the law were introduced through this Act in 1999:

- a change to the definition of who is able to give evidence
- physical measures to reduce the stress of giving evidence (such as informal dress, screens, live link CCTV and the use of pre-recording)
- restrictions on who can ask the witness questions
- restrictions on what sexual information about the witness is considered relevant in a trial
- restrictions on publishing information that could identify a witness.

Section 29 of this Act introduces the intermediary who will examine the witness. The court will approve the intermediary, but it is important that they can form a bond with the client and be able to understand and communicate precisely what they are saying.

Six pathfinder projects implemented the intermediary special measure between February 2004 and June 2005 – Merseyside, West Midlands, Thames Valley, South Wales, Norfolk and Devon and Cornwall, with the aim of rolling out the programme nationally after evaluation, which is now happening. If you support someone who needs an intermediary, the police or a lawyer will be able to contact one for you.

Under the Youth Justice and Criminal Evidence Act's special measures, people with learning disabilities could give evidence unsworn. This will support more people to be able to give evidence without having to be put under the pressure of a court situation.

Further information

Clare I and Murphy G, 'Witnesses with learning disabilities', *British Journal of Learning Disabilities*, vol 29, no 3 (2001).

Murphy G and Clare I, Adults' capacity to make legal decisions, in Bull R and Carson D, *Handbook of Psychology in Legal Contexts* (Wiley, 2003).

Office for Criminal Justice Reform, *Helping Witnesses Communicate: Guidance for Witnesses about the Intermediary Scheme* (Office for Criminal Justice Reform, 2004).

Plotnikoff J and Woolfson R, *The 'Go-between': Evaluation of Intermediary Pathfinders Projects* (Lexicon Limited, 2005).

Youth Justice and Criminal Evidence Act 1999 (see www.opsi.gov.uk).

Voice UK (see Question 3).

Why do we need all these laws? Aren't they just stopping people from having sex?

S ometimes staff worry about the laws about sexual activity, and don't want their clients (or themselves) to get into trouble, so they make sure that nobody in their care has any sexual relationships. This is an unsatisfactory situation, usually due to a misunderstanding of the law.

Laws are there to protect all of us from sex that we do not want, and especially to protect vulnerable people from abuse and exploitation.

The law makes it clear that sex with someone who cannot consent is a crime, but it also confirms that everyone else is free to make their own choices so people with learning disabilities who have consented to sex will not be affected. So the law protects the freedom and rights of people with learning disabilities as well as preventing abuse.

What the law, good practice and guidance say ...

Earlier law on sex offences was archaic and incoherent – it was also discriminatory. It provided little protection for men, and the laws aimed at the protection of people with learning disabilities were not comprehensive and the sentencing unjust.

Sexual crime, and the fear of sexual crime, has a profound and damaging effect on individuals and the social fabric of communities, and the incidence of people with learning disabilities as victims rightly causes alarm. Recent high profile cases have caused widespread public concern about the dangers that some sex offenders pose to the community in general, and to vulnerable people in particular.

It has been difficult to get convictions for sexual offences that have been carried out against people with learning disabilities. There needs to be more support and guidance for people to be able to give evidence in court and for more convictions to be brought. The change in the rape and sexual assault laws to make it clearer that these apply to people who do not have the capacity to consent should mean that it is easier to bring charges where offences have been committed.

This has already provided more protection for people with learning disabilities, enabling them to engage in consensual sexual activity while ensuring the incidence of abuse is reduced.

Putting it into practice

This section is designed for staff to use in practical settings: for example, with colleagues, managers or service users in training, staff meetings or other sessions. It brings together some resource materials that we currently use at **fpa**, which we hope will be of use to you.

The following pages in this section are designed to be photocopied and used with groups.

Sex and the law quiz

All **fpa** training aims to demystify the law for participants. When working in the area of sexual health and sex and relationships education, staff need a solid knowledge of the law to enable them to carry out their roles with confidence.

fpa training uses a sex and the law quiz, tailored to each particular course, which we have found to be an interesting, involving way to investigate the legal system and current legislation.

The following quiz is a very short version using some of the questions asked in **fpa**'s learning disability training courses. It is designed for use by or with staff who have no or little experience of the law.

The exercise

Materials needed

- One copy of the quiz for all participants and trainer.
- One copy of the answers for all participants and trainer.
- Pens.
- Overhead or PowerPoint projector and slides.

Time needed

- Between half an hour and one hour.

Give out a copy of the quiz to each person in the group and ask them to answer as many questions as they can by themselves. If group members are anxious, explain that they are not expected to know the answers. When they have finished ask them to discuss their answers with the person next to them for five minutes.

In the next 20–30 minutes go through the questions with the group (using the answer sheet) and allow time for discussion. Afterwards give all participants a copy of the answers to take away with them.

This exercise may have potential for conflict in that people often feel the law is unfair and may know of cases where the outcome is very different from the written statutes of legislation. It may be worth mentioning this beforehand to avoid controversy.

You may find some of the overhead projector/PowerPoint slides useful for the feedback part of this exercise (see page 97).

Sex and the law quiz

1. How old do you have to be to have sex, by law?

   a) 13   b) 16   c) 18   d) 21

2. If you have sex with someone who does not or cannot consent, is it rape?

   yes ☐   no ☐   unsure ☐

3. If you show your genitals by accident, can you be prosecuted for indecent exposure?

   yes ☐   no ☐   unsure ☐

4. Is it against the law for a care worker to have sex with someone with a learning disability whom they care for?

   yes ☐   no ☐   unsure ☐

5. Is it against the law to threaten, trick or bribe someone into having sex, if they have a learning disability or some other mental disorder?

   yes ☐   no ☐   unsure ☐

6. Is it possible for someone to be sterilised against their will?

   yes ☐   no ☐   unsure ☐

7. If you teach someone with a learning disability to masturbate, are you likely to be prosecuted?

   yes ☐   no ☐   unsure ☐

fpa © 2009

Sex and the law quiz answers

1. How old do you have to be to have sex, by law?

a) 13   b) 16   c) 18   d) 21

You must be 16 or over by law to have sex, regardless of the sex of your partner: this is the age of consent. The age of 13 is also important in law.

a) under 13
If the young person is under the age of 13, whether or not they consented to the activity does not matter. A young person under 13 does not, under any circumstances, have the legal capacity to consent to any form of sexual activity.

b) under 16
In the case of 13–15 year olds there is a potential defence where the defendant must prove that they reasonably believed that the young person was aged 16 or over.

In both of these cases judgement will be used where the defendant is under 18.

c) and d) 18 and 21
These are age ranges which used to apply in law to homosexual activity. The age was equalised at 16 for all sexual activity in 2000.

2. If you have sex with someone who does not or cannot consent, is it rape?

yes ✗   no ☐   unsure ☐

In England and Wales, the Sexual Offences Act 2003 defines rape as intentional penetration:

● of vagina, anus or mouth

● with a penis

● without consent (and reasonable belief of no consent)

● or of someone under 13.

Changes in the law through the Sexual Offences Act 2003 mean that having sex with someone who cannot consent is rape.

3. **If you show your genitals by accident, can you be prosecuted for indecent exposure?**

yes ☐   no ✖   unsure ☐

It is the intent which is the defining factor. It is an offence *[Sexual Offences Act 2003]* if someone intentionally exposes their genitals with the intention that another person will see them and be caused alarm or distress. This only applies to genitals; bottoms and breasts are not included (although these could be covered by a public order offence).

4. **Is it against the law for a care worker to have sex with someone with a learning disability whom they care for?**

yes ✖   no ☐   unsure ☐

It is an offence for care workers to engage in any form of sexual activity with the people that they care for. The definition of 'care worker' is wide and includes all health and social care staff whether full- or part-time, paid or voluntary. It also includes those in regular face-to-face contact with the client who involve themselves in aspects of their care such as the caretaker of a home, the cleaner or the gardener.

5. **Is it against the law to threaten, trick or bribe someone into having sex, if they have a learning disability or some other mental disorder?**

yes ✖   no ☐   unsure ☐

These offences *[Sexual Offences Act 2003]* are aimed at people with learning disabilities who can give consent to sexual activity but may be more susceptible with encouragement from others. This offence would include situations such as the perpetrator:

● threatening to hurt a family member if the person did not engage in a sexual activity

● lying to the person, saying that all friends do this kind of thing

● offering the person something – money, cigarettes or the promise of marriage or a favour.

6. Is it possible for someone to be sterilised against their will?

yes ☐　　　　　no ✘　　　　　unsure ☐

No operation may be performed on an adult without his or her consent.

However, if someone is not competent to make this decision for themselves then a decision by the court must be sought. This process involves the person on whom the operation would be carried out being represented by an Official Solicitor. The purpose of the process is to establish whether or not the proposed sterilisation is in the best interests of the patient. The evidence which needs to be provided is extensive and covers everything from proof that the patient cannot make their own decisions to proof that all less drastic measures of contraception have been tried.

7. If you teach someone with a learning disability to masturbate, are you likely to be prosecuted?

yes ☐　　　　　no ✘　　　　　unsure ☐

It depends on the way it is taught. If it is taught using diagrams and descriptions with no physical contact then it is fine as long as it is part of that person's agreed care plan. Touching a man's or woman's genitals could be interpreted as sexual touching which may be covered under offences from the Sexual Offences Act 2003.

The key would be whether a reasonable person would consider the touching to be sexual or not and the argument against the case of assisted masturbation is that the touching is generally going to be perceived as such.

It would have to be established that the activity cannot be explained to some people with a learning disability without using a hands-on method, that that method is identified by a multi-disciplinary care group as the right step to take at that particular time, and that the group identifies the person to do it and how it is to be done.

fpa © 2009

Overhead projector/ PowerPoint slides

The following slides are designed to be of use if you are speaking to other staff about the law or they could be used to support the feedback section of the sex and the law quiz. They are all slides that we find essential when running training.

You can either photocopy these slides onto acetate for use on an overhead projector or retype them into PowerPoint.

Definition of consent

A person consents if he agrees by choice, and has the freedom and capacity to make that choice.

Definition of sexual

An activity is sexual if a reasonable person would either always consider it to be sexual because of its nature, for example oral sex, or that it may be deemed to be sexual depending on the circumstances and intention. For example, a medical examination in a doctor's surgery, where the purpose is not sexual, would not be considered an assault.

Slide 3:

Sexual offences against persons with a mental disorder impeding choice
Sexual Offences Act 2003

Section 30: Sexual activity with a person with a mental disorder impeding choice.

Section 31: Causing or inciting a person, with a mental disorder impeding choice, to engage in sexual activity.

Section 32: Engaging in sexual activity in the presence of a person with a mental disorder impeding choice.

Section 33: Causing a person, with a mental disorder impeding choice, to watch a sexual act.

Slide 4:

Inducements to people with a mental disorder
Sexual Offences Act 2003

Section 34: Inducement, threat or deception to procure sexual activity with a person with a mental disorder.

Section 35: Causing a person with a mental disorder to engage in or agree to engage in sexual activity by inducement, threat or deception.

Section 36: Engaging in sexual activity in the presence, procured by inducement, threat or deception, of a person with a mental disorder.

Section 37: Causing a person with a mental disorder to watch a sexual act by inducement, threat or deception.

Slide 5:

Care workers for people with a mental disorder
Sexual Offences Act 2003

Section 38: Care workers: sexual activity with a person with a mental disorder.

Section 39: Care workers: causing or inciting sexual activity.

Section 40: Care workers: sexual activity in the presence of a person with a mental disorder.

Section 41: Care workers: causing a person with a mental disorder to watch a sexual act.

Slide 6:

Definition of care worker
Sexual Offences Act 2003 Section 42

● Workers from care/community/voluntary/ children's homes.

● Workers from NHS services or independent medical agencies.

● People in regular face-to-face contact with client, regardless of whether they provide physical or mental care.

● Paid or unpaid, full- or part-time.

Other rules/ethics

- International and European laws/rules.
- National laws.
- Religious rules.
- Professional codes of conduct.
- Regional or local guidelines.
- Employers' policies and guidelines.
- Local society's expectations.
- Family and cultural expectations.
- House rules for individual workplaces or living places.
- Custom and practice of staff.
- Service users' expectations.

Human Rights Act: easy guide

The Human Rights Act came into force in October 2000. It does not create any new rights, but provides a way for cases to be heard in UK courts or tribunals that may previously have had to go to the European Court of Human Rights. The Act is not designed to be used to bring actions against private individuals. For people with learning disabilities, the Act should reinforce a 'rights culture', ensuring that people working to support people with learning disabilities recognise the need to ensure that everyone receives the benefit of the law.

CASE STUDY

X and Y v The Netherlands [1985]
8 EHRR 235

X complained to the police about a sexual assault on his daughter, Y, a 16-year-old girl with a learning disability. The girl was resident in a private home, and the son-in-law of the director, who lived there with his wife, allegedly woke the girl up one night, took her to his room and forced her to get undressed and have sex.

The police decided not to prosecute provided the accused did not offend again. The father appealed against this decision but was told that as the girl could not make the complaint herself no one was entitled to do so on her behalf.

The applicants complained to the Human Rights Commission of breaches of Articles 3, 8, 13 and 14. A breach of Article 8 was agreed but not a breach of 3. It was felt that the breach of 8 covered the situation and that Articles 13 and 14 did not need assessing.

The case was referred to court on the breach of Article 8 by the Commission.

Article 8

1. Everyone has the right to respect for his private and family life, his home and his correspondence.

2. There shall be no interference by a public authority with the exercise of this right except such as is in accordance with the law and is necessary in a democratic society in the interests of national security, public safety or the economic wellbeing of the country, for the prevention of disorder or crime, for the protection of health or morals, or for the protection of the rights and freedoms of others.

The court decided that there had been a violation of Article 8, by lack of respect to the girl's private (including sexual) life by the authorities ignoring the claims of sexual assault. The State was ordered to pay 3,000 Dutch guilders to the girl.

It is important that the people that you work with know about their rights, and the Human Rights Act. For that reason, the handout on the next two pages is designed to be used with service users. It could also be used with staff as a brief introduction to the Human Rights Act. www.bild.org.uk has a comprehensive handout which could also be given to staff.

Not all articles of the European Convention on Human Rights were incorporated into UK legislation therefore not all articles are listed on the handout.

Human Rights Act

The Articles and Protocols of the Human Rights Act cover some of the following rights and freedoms. Articles and Protocols are legal statements, explaining the different rights contained in the Act.

Protocol 1, Article 1
No one has the right to unlawfully interfere with your possessions

Protocol 1, Article 2
Right to access to education

Article 2
The right to life

Article 3
No torture, inhuman or degrading treatment

Article 4
No slavery or enforced labour

Article 5
The right to liberty and personal freedom

Article 6
The right to a fair trial

Article 7
No punishment without law

Article 8
The right to privacy and family life

BILD © 2009

Article 9
Freedom of thought and religion

Article 10
Freedom of expression

Article 11
Freedom of assembly (meeting others)

Article 12
The right to marry and have a family

Article 14
Freedom from discrimination

Article 17
No one has the right to destroy or abuse rights

Policies and guidelines

Policies and guidelines help everyone to know where they stand when working on sensitive and sometimes controversial topics. These can range from national guidance on good practice, to local authority policy documents, to 'house rules' for individual homes and centres. Sex and relationships is an area in which there are often strongly held personal views, as well as great potential for both harm and scandal. Clear guidelines will protect people with learning disabilities, promote their rights and at the same time support carers in their role and prevent agencies from making avoidable mistakes. Because of the nature of sex and relationships work, it is advisable to have a clear, supportive, flexible policy not only for the protection of clients and staff, but to provide support to clients for this sensitive area of their lives.

The following is not intended as a handout but as a point of reference and guidelines to be considered and followed when developing policy.

It is based on guidance from the National Assembly for Wales on sexual health and looked after children.[10]

Commitments we support

The **Human Rights Act** (1998) states that it is everyone's right to have a private life and a family.

Valuing People (2001) from the Department of Health states that people with learning disabilities have a right to sex and relationships education (SRE) and good, accessible information about growing up.

Valuing People Now (2008) was a consultation held to seek people's views on the priorities for the learning disability agenda over three years following on from Valuing People in 2001. These priorities form the basis of a plan for 2009–2011.

The Department of Health issued the **No Secrets** (2000) guidance which encourages all responsible agencies to work together to ensure a coherent policy for the protection of vulnerable adults at risk of abuse.

---

[10] National Assembly for Wales, *Sexual Health and Looked After Children* (National Assembly for Wales, 2008).

The issues at a glance

- SRE can protect vulnerable people from abuse and support their rights as sexual beings.

- People undertaking SRE with people with learning disabilities have in the past worked unsupported and without national and local guidance. This has prevented many staff and carers from attempting this essential but challenging work.

- Sexual behaviour is often poorly dealt with in people with learning disabilities. Over-protection and concerns about the risks involved means that they can be denied their rights and enough privacy for normal exploration, while under-protection can lead to sexual exploitation, such as abusive relationships.

- There is widespread misunderstanding of the legal issues relating to sexual behaviour. Some social services departments and care organisations wrongly believe that any sexual activity by someone with a learning disability, however consenting and non-exploitative, is automatically against the law.

- The lack of clarity over confidentiality leaves people with learning disabilities unsure about where they can get advice about sexual health without the details being reported back to their parents/carers.

- The non-accessible nature of some services and information about sexual health can leave people with learning disabilities unsure of whether that service or information applies to them.

"I am not sure what I am allowed to do or say and I am not sure if my managers will support me." **Residential social worker**

"I don't know where to start, they all have such different abilities." **Teacher**

"What if they go out and start experimenting because of what we teach them?" **Care home staff**

What action should we take?

Whatever level the policy is for, whether for one house or the whole county, you need to go through the same steps. The length of what you write and what it contains will be different according to the setting.

- **Consult** the people who will be using the policy, and also the people with learning disabilities they care for.

- Agree where you stand on **beliefs and rights**, for example equality of opportunity.

- **Identify** where guidance is needed, and any **gaps or out-of-date parts of existing guidance**, and set out what should be done in each situation.

- Don't be afraid to include **controversial issues**: these are just the kind of areas where guidance is needed and often include pornography, support for gay, lesbian and bisexual service users, sexual behaviour, consent, risk and inappropriate masturbation.

- Decide how **SRE** will be provided to those who miss out at school, and who will deliver it. This will be an important part of most policies.

- Be completely clear about the rules on **confidentiality**, what needs to be recorded and reported, and how these link to other local responsibilities, such as policies and procedures for vulnerable adults. Everyone needs to know where they stand, including the people with learning disabilities.

- Set out what **other policies** relate to this one, and make sure they all fit together with no contradictions.

- Work out how you will **let everyone know** about the policy, and how you will help them understand it and want to follow it. It may be that some training is needed for staff and you may choose to produce an additional, accessible policy for the people that you work with to support them.

- Decide who will **check** that it is working and when it will be **reviewed**.

Sample framework for a policy and guidelines document

The following sections could be included in a policy and guidelines document:

Policy: where do we stand?

The rights and responsibilities of people with learning disabilities.
The rights and responsibilities of staff and carers.
The law.
Balancing risk and protection.
Equality and challenging discrimination.

Guidelines for staff: what should we do?

Involving parents/carers and families.
Consent and capacity to consent.
Advocacy.
Confidentiality and privacy.
Intimate care, hygiene and touching.
Talking about growing up and sex.
Personal and sexual relationships and behaviour.
Sexual preferences, for example homosexuality.
Pornography and pin-ups.
Contraception and sexual health.
SRE.
Sexual abuse.
Counselling, advice and therapy.
Staff training.

Where to find more help

About the law.
Related local policies.
Local sexual health services.

"I used to be scared to raise the issue in case I was opening a can of worms. Now that I know where I stand and that I will get support I will be much happier to talk about sex with the people I work with."
Residential social worker, after a training course about a new policy

The law in more detail

This section is for those who wish to have more background information about the law in general or want some more details about the offences described in this publication. It may be useful for anyone intending to carry out training in this area, those developing policies and as a reference point to more detailed information.

Defining learning disability

This section defines the term 'learning disability' as it was used in the Sexual Offences Act 2003, which was included in the definition of 'mental disorder' in the Mental Health Act 1983:

> *"mental illness, arrested or incomplete development of mind, psychopathic disorder and any other disorder or disability of mind."*

This was then amended by the Mental Health Act 2007 which has defined it as:

> *"any disorder or disability of the mind."*

The 2007 Act removes the four sub categories of mental disorder and also states that someone with a learning disability does not automatically have a mental disorder when looking at issues of detention or guardianship orders.

Definitions in the Mental Capacity Act 2005 are slightly different. The Mental Capacity Act refers to any individual who at the time of a decision is unable to make that decision because of *an impairment of, or a disturbance in the functioning of, the mind or brain*.

The sources and process of law

Sources of law

Two of the sources of law in England and Wales are case law and statute law.

Case law (or common law) is law which is developed through decisions by judges necessary to decide the cases brought before them. Statute law (or legislation) comes from Acts of Parliament and is the commonest source of new laws. Most judgements are based upon a consideration of statute and case law.

Our legal system divides our laws into two categories: civil and criminal. Each one serves a very different purpose. The civil law deals with the rights and duties of one individual to another. The criminal law is concerned with establishing social order and protecting the community as a whole. It gives us a set of rules for peaceful, orderly and safe living.

Broadly speaking in the area of people's sexual behaviour we are concerned with criminal law.

There are other influences, such as the European Convention on Human Rights, which have been incorporated into law. This means that domestic courts must take full account of their provisions when considering a grievance.

The process of law

There are many stages that a case must go through if prosecution is to succeed, and many people who are involved in the process.

1. When a case is brought to the police they investigate and decide whether there is enough evidence to take the case forward and whether it is in the public interest to do so.

2. When this is determined, the case file is passed to the Crown Prosecution Service which makes a decision in accordance with the Code of Crown Prosecutors. This Code is a public document and available to anyone on www.cps.gov.uk.

3. There are two stages in the decision to prosecute.

    ● The first stage is the **evidential test** where the Crown Prosecutors must be satisfied that there is enough evidence to provide a realistic prospect of conviction against each defendant on each charge. The evidence must be reliable, therefore a case may not proceed if the complainant would not be competent to give evidence (although there is legislation in place to support vulnerable witnesses: see Question 31).

- The second stage is the **public interest test** which will only be used if there is enough evidence. This test is whether it is in the public interest to prosecute the defendant.

4. If both these tests are met the case will proceed to court.

5. The defendant will either be found guilty, and be sentenced by the judge, or not guilty for the offence.

Offences and sentencing

This table is adapted from Appendix 2, Table of changes, in Stevenson K, Davies A and Gunn M, *Blackstone's Guide to the Sexual Offences Act 2003* (Oxford University Press, 2004).

Note: 'MP' = maximum penalty.

Sexual Offences Act (SOA) 2003	Offences prior to the SOA 2003
Rape Vaginal, anal or oral penetration with penis *MP: life* **Rape of a child under 13** Vaginal, anal or oral *MP: life*	**Rape** [SOA 1956] Vaginal or anal penetration with penis *MP: life*
Assault by penetration Vaginal or anal penetration with object *MP: life* **Sexual assault** Sexual touching *MP: 10 years* **Assault of a child under 13 by penetration** Vaginal or anal penetration with object *MP: life* **Sexual assault of a child under 13** Sexual touching *MP: 14 years*	**Indecent assault (on a woman)** [SOA 1956] *MP: 10 years* **Indecent assault (on a man)** [SOA 1956] *MP: 10 years*
Trespass with intent to commit a sexual offence *MP: 10 years*	**Trespass with intent to commit rape** [Theft Act 1968] *MP: 14 years (in home), 10 years (other)*

Sexual Offences Act (SOA) 2003	Offences prior to the SOA 2003
Committing an offence with intent to commit a sexual offence *MP: life (with kidnapping), 10 years (other)*	**Assault with intent to commit buggery** [SOA 1956] *MP: 10 years* **Abduction of a woman** [SOA 1956] *MP: 14 years* **Abduction of an unmarried girl under 18** [SOA 1956] *MP: 2 years* **Abduction of a defective** [SOA 1956] *MP: 2 years*
Administering a substance with intent To enable sexual activity *MP: 10 years*	**Administering drugs to a woman to obtain or facilitate intercourse** [SOA 1956] *MP: 2 years*
Rape of a child under 13 *MP: life* **Assault of a child under 13 by penetration** *MP: life*	**Sexual intercourse with a girl under 13** [SOA 1956] *MP: life* **Buggery** [SOA 1956] Anal intercourse with child under age of consent *MP: life*
Sexual activity with a child *MP: 14 years where defendant is 18 or over, otherwise 5 years*	**Sexual intercourse with a girl under 16** [SOA 1956] *MP: 2 years* **Buggery** [SOA 1956] *MP: life*

Sexual Offences Act (SOA) 2003	Offences prior to the SOA 2003
Rape of a child under 13 *MP: life* **Assault of child under 13 by penetration** *MP: life* **Sexual assault of child under 13** *MP: 14 years* **Causing or inciting a child under 13 to engage in sexual activity** *MP: life where penetration occurs, otherwise 14 years* **Sexual activity with a child** *MP: 14 years where defendant is 18 or over, otherwise 5 years* **Causing or inciting a child to engage in sexual activity** *MP: 14 years where defendant is 18 or over, otherwise 5 years* **Engaging in sexual activity in the presence of a child** *MP: 10 years where defendant is 18 or over, otherwise 5 years* **Causing a child to watch a sexual act** *MP: 10 years where defendant is 18 or over, otherwise 5 years*	**Indecency with child under 16** [Indecency with Children Act 1960] *MP: 10 years*
Arranging or facilitating commission of a child sex offence *MP: 14 years*	NEW
Meeting a child following sexual grooming etc *MP: 10 years*	NEW

Sexual Offences Act (SOA) 2003	Offences prior to the SOA 2003
Risk of sexual harm order (RSHO) *If breached: 5 years*	NEW
Rape of a child under 13 *MP: life* **Assault of a child under 13 by penetration** *MP: life* **Sexual assault of a child under 13** *MP: 14 years* **Causing or inciting a child under 13 to engage in sexual activity** *MP: life where penetration occurs, otherwise 14 years* **Sexual activity with a child family member** *MP: 14 years where defendant is 18 or over, otherwise 5 years* **Inciting a child family member to engage in sexual activity** *MP: 14 years where defendant is 18 or over, otherwise 5 years* **Sex with an adult relative: penetration** *MP: 2 years* **Sex with an adult relative: consenting to penetration** *MP: 2 years*	**Incest** [SOA 1956] *MP: life where victim is under 13, otherwise 7 years*
Inciting a child family member to engage in sexual activity *MP: 14 years where defendant is 18 or over, otherwise 5 years*	**Incitement of girls under 16 to commit incest** [Criminal Law Act 1977] *MP: 2 years*

Sexual Offences Act (SOA) 2003	Offences prior to the SOA 2003
Sexual activity with a child family member *MP: 14 years where defendant is 18 or over, otherwise 5 years* **Sex with an adult relative: penetration** *MP: 2 years* **Sex with an adult relative: consenting to penetration** *MP: 2 years*	**Incest by a woman** [SOA 1956] *MP: 7 years*
Abuse of position of trust *MP: 5 years*	**Abuse of trust** [SO(A)A 2000] *MP: 5 years*
Sexual activity with a person with a mental disorder impeding choice *MP: life where penetration occurs, otherwise 14 years* **Causing or inciting a person, with a mental disorder impeding choice, to engage in sexual activity** *MP: life where penetration occurs, otherwise 14 years* **Engaging in sexual activity in the presence of a person with a mental disorder, impeding choice** *MP: 10 years* **Causing a person, with a mental disorder impeding choice, to watch a sexual act** *MP: 10 years*	**Intercourse with a defective** [SOA 1956] *MP: 2 years*

Sexual Offences Act (SOA) 2003	Offences prior to the SOA 2003
Inducement, threat or deception to procure sexual activity with a person with a mental disorder *MP: life where penetration occurs, otherwise 14 years*	
Causing a person with a mental disorder to engage in or agree to engage in sexual activity by inducement, threat or deception *MP: life where penetration occurs, otherwise 14 years*	
Engaging in sexual activity in the presence, procured by inducement, threat or deception, of a person with a mental disorder *MP: 10 years*	
Causing a person with a mental disorder to watch a sexual act by inducement, threat or deception *MP: 10 years*	
Care workers: sexual activity with a person with a mental disorder *MP: 14 years where penetration occurs, otherwise 10 years*	**Sexual intercourse with patients** [Mental Health Act 1959] *MP: 2 years*
Care workers: causing or inciting sexual activity *MP: 14 years where penetration occurs, otherwise 10 years*	
Care workers: sexual activity in the presence of a person with a mental disorder *MP: 7 years*	

Sexual Offences Act (SOA) 2003	Offences prior to the SOA 2003
Care workers: causing a person with a mental disorder to watch a sexual act *MP: 7 years*	
Inducement, threat or deception to procure sexual activity with a person with a mental disorder *MP: life where penetration occurs, otherwise 14 years* **Causing a person with a mental disorder to engage in or agree to engage in sexual activity by inducement, threat or deception** *MP: life where penetration occurs, otherwise 14 years*	**Procurement of sexual intercourse from a woman by threat or intimidation** [SOA 1956] *MP: 2 years* **Procurement of intercourse from a woman by false pretences or false representations** [SOA 1956] *MP: 2 years*
WHERE PERSON BEING PROSTITUTED IS OVER 18 **Causing or inciting prostitution for gain** *MP: 7 years* **Controlling prostitution for gain** *MP: 7 years*	**Causing prostitution of women** [SOA 1956] *MP: 2 years* **Procuration of girl under 21** [SOA 1956] *MP: 2 years* **Causing or encouraging prostitution of a defective** [SOA 1956] *MP: 2 years* **Man living on the earnings of prostitution** [SOA 1956] *MP: 7 years* **Living on the earnings of male prostitution** [SOA 1967] *MP: 7 years* **Woman exercising control over a prostitute** [SOA 1956] *MP: 7 years*

Sexual Offences Act (SOA) 2003	Offences prior to the SOA 2003
WHERE PERSON BEING PROSTITUTED IS UNDER 18 **Paying for sexual services of a child** *MP: life (child under 13), 14 years (child under 16 with penetration), otherwise 7 years* **Causing or inciting child prostitution or pornography** *MP: 14 years* **Controlling a child prostitute or a child involved in pornography** *MP: 14 years* **Arranging or facilitating child prostitution or pornography** *MP: 14 years*	**Causing and encouraging prostitution of (etc) a girl under 16** *MP: 2 years* **Procuration of girl under 21** *MP: 2 years* **Causing or encouraging prostitution of a defective** [SOA 1956] *MP: 2 years* **Man living on the earnings of prostitution** [SOA 1956] *MP: 7 years* **Living on the earnings of male prostitution** [SOA 1967] *MP: 7 years* **Woman exercising control over a prostitute** [SOA 1956] *MP: 7 years*
Trafficking into the UK for sexual exploitation *MP: 14 years* **Trafficking within the UK for sexual exploitation** *MP: 14 years* **Trafficking out of the UK for sexual exploitation** *MP: 14 years*	**Traffic in prostitution** [Nationality, Immigration and Asylum Act 2002] *MP: 14 years*
REPEALED	**Solicitation by men** [SOA 1956] *MP: 2 years*
REFRAMED SO AS TO BE GENDER NEUTRAL *MP: fine*	**Loitering or soliciting for the purposes of prostitution** [Street Offences Act 1959] *MP: fine*

Sexual Offences Act (SOA) 2003	Offences prior to the SOA 2003
REFRAMED SO AS TO BE GENDER NEUTRAL *MP: fine*	**Kerb crawling** [SOA 1985] *MP: fine*
REFRAMED SO AS TO BE GENDER NEUTRAL *MP: fine*	**Persistent soliciting of women for the purposes of prostitution** [SOA 1985] *MP: fine*
Exposure *MP: 2 years*	**Indecent exposure** [Vagrancy Act 1824, Town and Police Clauses Act 1847] *MP: 3 months*
Voyeurism *MP: 2 years*	NEW
Sexual penetration of a corpse *MP: 2 years*	NEW
Intercourse with an animal *MP: 2 years*	**Buggery** (bestiality) [SOA 1956] *MP: 2 years*
Sexual activity in a public lavatory *MP: 6 months or a fine*	**S5 Public Order Act 1986** *MP: fine* **Outraging public decency** *Common law offence*
OFFENCES REPEALED WHERE IT CONCERNS CONSENSUAL BEHAVIOUR BETWEEN ADULTS	**Buggery** [SOA 1956] *MP: 2 years* **Gross indecency** [SOA 1956] *MP: 2 years* **Procuring others to commit homosexual acts** [SOA 1956] *MP: 2 years*

Relevant Acts of Parliament and rules

Sometimes it is useful to know the background of where legislation comes from and the context in which it arose. The following is a list of Acts of Parliament and other rules which concern people with learning disabilities and sexual offences. This list is not exhaustive but is a starting point for anyone wishing to research the legislation further. Good places to start are the Parliament, Stationery Office and Home Office websites:

- www.parliament.uk
- www.homeoffice.gov.uk
- www.opsi.gov.uk

Abortion Act 1967

Care Standards Act 2000

Children Act 1989, 2004

Civil Partnership Act 2004

Criminal Justice Act 1988

Criminal Justice and Courts Services Act 2000

Criminal Justice and Immigration Act 2008

Criminal Justice and Public Order Act 1994

Disability Discrimination Act 2005

Education Act 1996

Education (No 2) Act 1986

Employment and Training Act 1973

Employment Rights Act 1996

Family Law Reform Act 1969

Forced Marriage Civil Protection Act 2007

Gender Recognition Act 2004

Human Fertilisation and Embryology Act 2008

Human Rights Act 1998

Learning and Skills Act 2000

Local Government Act 1986

Matrimonial Causes Act 1973

Mental Capacity Act 2005

Mental Health Act 1959, 1983, 2007

Mental Health (Amendment) Act 1982

Mental Health Act Code of Practice 1983

National Health Service Act 1977

NHS Trusts and Primary Care Trusts (Sexually Transmitted Diseases) Directions 2000

No Secrets 2000

Protection of Children Act 1978

Public Interest Disclosure Act 1998

Sexual Offences Act 1956, 1967, 1985, 1993, 2003

Sexual Offences (Amendment) Act 1992, 2000

Youth Justice and Criminal Evidence Act 1999

Relevant case law

As all law in England and Wales is made up of statute and case law, it is often interesting to look at some cases to see if their outcomes affected legislation. Unfortunately there is very little case law in this area, as very few cases get to the court stage. This list is a summary of some of the cases we have mentioned throughout the publication and some that we have not.

If you are a newcomer to legal literature the references below relate to the publications you can find them in.

They contain a case name, for example:

R v Bellamy

and the year of prosecution or appeal, for example:

[1985]

and a publication reference, for example:

82 Criminal Appeals Report 222

The above reference means that it is in the number 82 Criminal Appeals Report on page 222.

You may want to go to a specialist law library and look these references up, but most can also be accessed on the internet. Some good websites are:

British and Irish Legal Information Institute – www.bailii.org

World Legal Information Institute – www.worldlii.org

Lexis Nexis, legal resources – www.lexisnexis.co.uk

Re B (a minor) (wardship: sterilisation) [1987] 2 All England Law Reports 206

A case about sterilisation of a 17-year-old woman.

R v Bellamy [1985] 82 Criminal Appeals Report 222

A case of rape where both parties had a mild learning disability, and they were sexual partners.

R v Bromiley [2000] Times Law Reports 4 July

A 37-year-old female care assistant convicted of indecent assault on five learning disabled boys aged 12–14.

R v Brough [1996] England and Wales Court of Appeal Criminal Division 236

Male with mild learning disabilities, had relationship with 12-year-old girl who became pregnant.

R v Cash [2004] England and Wales Court of Appeal Criminal Division 666

An appeal case where male with learning disabilities was convicted as an accomplice to kidnap and rape where his disability was not recognised in the initial trial.

Re D (a minor) (wardship: sterilisation) [1976] Law Reports: Family Division 185

Sterilisation of an 11-year-old girl with Sotos Syndrome.

R v Deakin [1994] 4 All England Law Reports 769

A male care worker convicted of indecently assaulting a female client with Down's syndrome (no consent).

R v Evans [1998] England and Wales Court of Appeal Criminal Division 21

A male worker engaging in consensual sexual activity with a client convicted of indecent assault.

Gillick v West Norfolk & Wisbech Area Health Authority [1986] AC 112

Victoria Gillick, mother who wanted to stop her local authority being able to provide her under-16-year-old daughters with contraception without her knowledge.

R v Hall [1988] 86 Criminal Appeals Reports 159

Principal of residential college, convicted of assisting a severely disabled female student with masturbation.

R v Hassana Francis [2000] England and Wales Court of Appeal Criminal Division 58

Female cleaner accused of indecently assaulting a 16-year-old boy with cerebral palsy.

Lister & Ors (AP) v Hesley Hall [2001] United Kingdom House of Lords 22

A case of abuse of many boys in a boarding school by staff.

R v Hudson [1966] 1 Queens Bench 448

A 22-year-old man, where trial assessed whether he knew the girl he engaged in sexual activity with had a learning disability.

R v Goodwin [1995] Criminal Appeals Reports (Sentencing) 14

Male registered nurse convicted for a consensual sexual relationship with a mental health patient.

R v McDonagh [1998] England and Wales Court of Appeal Criminal Division 308

Father convicted of indecent assault on his learning disabled son.

R v Masih [1986] Criminal Law Review 395

A mildly learning disabled man convicted of rape, possibly encouraged by others.

R v Robinson [1994] 3 All England Law Reports 346

A 15-year-old girl with a learning disability claimed to have been raped by mother's lover.

R v X,Y,Z [1990] 91 Criminal Appeal Reports 36

A case where screens were used in the court to protect children and assist them in giving evidence.

X and Y v Netherlands [1985] 8 European Human Rights Reports 235

A Human Rights Act case.

Sex offenders notification requirements and orders

Notification requirements

The sex offenders register was introduced in 1997. Registration on the register is an automatic consequence of a conviction, fining or caution for an offence specified in Schedule 1 of the Sex Offenders Act 1997.

The Sexual Offences Act 2003 made the notification requirements for the register stronger and easier to enforce.

Anyone registered must now register again annually, regardless of whether their circumstances have changed. Failure to do so could result in five years' imprisonment.

A notification period is the length of time an offender must stay on the register. It is determined by the severity of the sentence imposed. Offenders sentenced to 30 months or more of imprisonment remain on the register for life. There are lesser periods for under 18s who sexually offend although it is possible for them to be put on the register for life.

Being on the register means the offender must notify the police three days after conviction, caution or release from prison of his name, date of birth and address. He must also inform the police of any change of address, or if he is staying anywhere other than his registered address for seven or more days, including holidays abroad.

The Act provides for 'sex tourists' convicted of sex crimes abroad to comply with the notification requirements. In addition there is a new foreign travel banning order that will enable courts, in certain circumstances, to prohibit those convicted of a sexual offence against a child under 16 from travelling abroad.

All notifications must be made in person, enabling the police to take photographs and fingerprints.

Orders

Sex Offender Orders (SOOs) are civil restraining orders designed to protect the public from harm. They can cover people convicted of sexual offences as well as anyone convicted of an offence which may cause sexual harm. There are two types: Sex Offences Prevention Orders (SOPOs) and Risk of Sexual Harm Orders (RSHOs).

RSHOs are new and specifically targeted at adults (over 18s) to prevent them engaging in sexual activity with children. SOPOs can be imposed on anyone aged ten or over who poses a risk of sexual harm to others. The minimum duration of both orders is five years and both can be renewed.

These orders are extremely wide-ranging and can be used to prohibit people making any contact with children, typically by preventing them going near schools, children's events or living anywhere that children live or visit. Courts can impose these civil orders but they have to be sure that they are protecting the public from serious sexual harm due to the possible infringement on civil liberties they present.

Bibliography

fpa publications and resources

Fanstone C and Katrak Z, *Sexuality and Learning Disability: A Resource for Staff* (**fpa**).

fpa, *All About Us* (CD-ROM) (**fpa**).

fpa, *Challenging Homophobia: Equality, Diversity, Inclusion* (**fpa**).

fpa, *Factsheet: Abortion* (**fpa**).

fpa, *Factsheet: Religion, Contraception and Abortion* (**fpa**).

fpa, *Factsheet: Sex and Relationships Education* (**fpa**).

fpa, *Factsheet: The Law on Sex* (**fpa**).

fpa, *Talking Together ... About Contraception* (**fpa**).

fpa, *Talking Together ... About Growing Up* (**fpa**).

fpa, *Talking together ... About Sex and Relationships* (**fpa**).

Gadd M and Hinchcliffe J, *Jiwsi: A Pick 'n' Mix of Sex and Relationships Education Activities* (**fpa**).

Simpson A, Lafferty A and McConkey R, *Out of the Shadows: "Our voices aren't going to go quietly into the shadows anymore"* (**fpa**).

fpa publications and resources can be purchased from **fpa** at www.fpa.org.uk or by calling 0845 122 8600 or emailing fpadirect@fpa.org.uk.

Abbot D and Howarth J, *Secret Loves, Hidden Lives? Exploring Issues for Men and Women with Learning Difficulties who are Gay, Lesbian or Bisexual* (The Policy Press, 2005).

Affleck F, *You and Your Baby 0–1 Years* (CHANGE, 2004).

Bartlett P and Sandland R, *Mental Health Law: Policy and Practice* (Oxford University Press, 2003).

British Medical Association, *Consent Toolkit* (British Medical Association, 2003).

British Medical Association and The Law Society, *Assessment of Mental Capacity: Guidance for Doctors and Lawyers* (BMJ Books, 2004).

British Institute of Learning Disabilities and the West Midlands Learning Disability Forum, *Social and Personal Relationships* (British Institute of Learning Disabilities, 2001).

Brown H, *Making Records Work: Recording with Care in Learning Disability Services* (Pavilion Publishing and Department of Health, 2001).

Brown H and Thompson D, 'Service responses to men with intellectual disabilities who have unacceptable or abusive sexual behaviours: the case against inaction', *Journal of Applied Research in Intellectual Disabilities*, vol 10, no 2 (1997), 176–197.

Calcraft R and Ann Craft Trust, *Blowing the Whistle on Abuse of Adults with Learning Disabilities* (Ann Craft Trust, 2005).

Cambridge P, *HIV, Sex and Learning Disability* (Pavilion Publishing, 1997).

Cambridge P, 'The HIV testing of a man with learning disabilities: informed consent, confidentiality, and policy', *Journal of Adult Protection*, vol 3, no 4 (2001), 23–28.

Cambridge P, *The Sexuality and Sexual Rights of People with Learning Disabilities: Considerations for Staff and Carers* (British Institute of Learning Disabilities, 1996).

Cambridge P and Carnaby S, 'A personal touch: managing the risks of abuse during intimate and personal care for people with learning disabilities', *Journal of Adult Protection*, vol 2, no 4 (2000), 4–16.

Cambridge P and Carnaby S, *Making it Personal: Providing Intimate and Personal Care for People with Learning Disabilities* (Pavilion Publishing, 2000).

Cambridge P, Carnaby S and McCarthy M, 'Responding to masturbation in supporting sexuality and challenging behaviour in services for people with learning disabilities', *Journal of Learning Disabilities*, vol 7, no 3 (2003), 251–266.

Clare I and Murphy G, 'Witnesses with learning disabilities', *British Journal of Learning Disabilities*, vol 29, no 3 (2001).

Contact a Family, *Growing Up, Sex and Relationships: A Booklet to Support Parents of Young Disabled People* (Contact a Family, 2005).

Craft A, *Practical Issues in Sexuality and Learning Disabilities* (Routledge, 1994).

Crown Prosecution Service, *Sexual Offences Act 2003* (Crown Prosecution Service, 2004).

Crown Prosecution Service, *The Code for Crown Prosecutors* (Crown Prosecution Service Communications Branch, 2004).

Davies L, *The Social Worker's Guide to Children and Families Law* (Jessica Kingsley Publishers, 2008).

Department for Children, Education, Lifelong Learning and Skills, *Personal and Social Education Framework for 7 to 19 Year Olds in Wales* (Welsh Assembly Government, 2008).

Department for Children, Schools and Families, *Enabling Young People to Access Contraceptive and Sexual Health Advice – Guidance for Youth Support Workers* (Department for Children, Schools and Families, 2005).

Department for Children, Schools and Families, *Enabling Young People to Access Contraceptive and Sexual Health Advice. Legal and Policy Framework for Social Workers, Residential Social Workers, Foster Carers and other Social Care Practitioners* (Department for Children, Schools and Families, 2005).

Department for Children, Schools and Families, *Government Response to the Report by the Sex and Relationships Education (SRE) Review Steering Group* (Department for Children, Schools and Families, 2008).

Department for Children, Schools and Families, *Safeguarding Children and Young People from Sexual Exploitation. Draft Guidance* (Department for Children, Schools and Families, 2008).

Department for Children, Schools and Families, *Working Together to Safeguard Children: A Guide to Inter-agency Working to Safeguard and Promote the Welfare of Children* (Department for Children, Schools and Families, 2006).

Department for Constitutional Affairs, Department of Health and Welsh Assembly Government, *Mental Capacity Act 2005 – Easy Read Summary* (Department of Health, 2006).

Department for Constitutional Affairs, Department of Health, Welsh Assembly Government and Public Guardianship Office, *Mental Capacity Act – Summary* (Department of Health, 2006).

Department for Education and Employment, *Sex and Relationships Education Guidance, Circular 0116/2000* (Department for Education and Employment, 2000).

Department of Health, *Best Practice Guidance for Doctors and Other Health Professionals on the Provision of Advice and Treatment to Young People Under 16 on Contraception, Sexual and Reproductive Health* (Department of Health, 2004).

Department of Health, *Consent: A Guide for People with Learning Disabilities* (Department of Health, 2001).

Department of Health, *Protection of Vulnerable Adults (POVA) Scheme in England and Wales for Care Homes and Domiciliary Care Agencies: A Practical Guide* (Department of Health, 2006).

Department of Health, *Reference Guide to Consent for Examination or Treatment* (Department of Health, 2001).

Department of Health, *Valuing People: A New Strategy for Learning Disability for the 21st Century – a White Paper* (Department of Health, 2001).

Department of Health, *Valuing People Now: From Progress to Transformation – a Consultation on the Next Three Years of Learning Disability Policy* (Department of Health, 2008).

Department of Health and Home Office, *No Secrets: Guidance on Developing and Implementing Multi-agency Policies and Procedures to Protect Vulnerable Adults from Abuse* (Department of Health and Home Office Communications Directorate, 2000).

Drury J, Hutchinson L and Wright J, *Holding On, Letting Go* (Souvenir Press, 2000).

Fairbairn G, Rowley D and Bowen M, *Sexuality, Learning Difficulties and Doing What's Right* (David Fulton Publishers, 1995).

Fallon P et al, *Report on the Committee of Inquiry into the Personality Disorder Unit, Ashworth Special Hospital* (The Stationery Office, 1999).

Fyson R, *Young People with Learning Disabilities who Show Sexually Inappropriate or Abusive Behaviours* (Ann Craft Trust, 2005).

General Medical Council, *Consent: Patients and Doctors Making Decisions Together* (General Medical Council, 2008).

Harbour A, *Children with Mental Disorder and the Law: A Guide to Law and Practice* (Jessica Kingsley Publishers, 2008).

Harney N, *Vulnerable Adult Abuse – Recent Developments in the Law* (Association of Child Abuse Lawyers, 2001).

Hingsburger D, *Hand Made Love: A Guide for Teaching about Male Masturbation* (Diverse City Press, 1995).

Hingsburger D and Haar S, *Finger Tips: A Guide for Teaching about Female Masturbation* (Diverse City Press, 2003).

Hingsburger D and Harber M, *The Ethics of Touch: Establishing and Maintaining Appropriate Boundaries in Service to People with Developmental Disabilities* (Diverse City Press, 1998).

Home Office, *A Choice by Right* (Home Office Communications Directorate, 2000).

Home Office, *Adults: Safer from Sexual Crime – the Sexual Offences Act 2003* (Home Office Communications Directorate, 2004).

Home Office, *Setting the Boundaries* (Home Office Communications Directorate, 2001).

Home Office, *Sexual Offences Act 2003* (Home Office Communications Directorate, 2004).

Home Office, *Working Within the Sexual Offences Act 2003 SOA/4* (Home Office Communications Directorate, 2004).

Hughes A and Coombs P, *Easy Guide to the Human Rights Act 1998* (British Institute of Learning Disabilities, 2001).

Lord Chancellor's Department, *Who Decides? Making Decisions on Behalf of Mentally Incapacitated Adults* (Her Majesty's Stationery Office, 1997).

Lovell E, *Children and Young People who Display Sexually Harmful Behaviour* (NSPCC Information Briefings, 2002).

Lovell E, *"I think I might need some more help with this problem": Responding to Children and Young People who Display Sexually Harmful Behaviour* (NSPCC, 2002).

McCarthy M, *Sexuality and Women with Learning Disabilities* (Jessica Kingsley Publishers, 1999).

McCarthy M and Thompson D, *Sex and the 3 Rs: Rights, Responsibilities and Risks* (Pavilion Publishing, 1998).

McGaw S, *Parent Assessment Manual 2.0* (Pill Creek Publishing, 2007).

McGaw S, *What Works for Parents with Learning Disabilities?* (Barnardo's, 2000).

Morris J, *The Right Support: Report on the Task Force on Supporting Disabled Adults in their Parenting Role* (Joseph Rowntree Foundation, 2003).

Murphy G, 'Capacity to consent to sexual relationships in adults with learning disabilities', *Journal of Family Planning and Reproductive Healthcare*, vol 29, no 3 (2003), 148–149.

Murphy G, Intellectual disabilities, sexual abuse and sexual offending, in Carr A et al, *Handbook of Intellectual Disability and Clinical Psychology Practice* (Routledge, 2007).

Murphy G and Clare I, Adults' capacity to make legal decisions, in Bull R and Carson D, *Handbook of Psychology in Legal Contexts* (Wiley, 2003).

National Assembly for Wales, *Personal and Social Education (PSE) and Work-Related Education (WRE) in the Basic Curriculum, Circular 13/03* (National Assembly for Wales, 2003).

National Assembly for Wales, *Sex and Relationships Education in Schools: Circular 11/02* (National Assembly for Wales, 2002).

National Assembly for Wales, *Sexual Health and Looked After Children* (National Assembly for Wales, 2003).

NHS Edinburgh and Lothian, *Making Choices, Keeping Safe: Policy and Practice Guidelines on Relationships and Sexual Wellbeing when Working with People with Learning Disabilities* (NHS Edinburgh and Lothian, 2004).

Nursing and Midwifery Council, *Record Keeping: Guidance for Nurses and Midwives* (Nursing and Midwifery Council, 2009).

Office for Criminal Justice Reform, *Helping Witnesses Communicate: Guidance for Witnesses about the Intermediary Scheme* (Office for Criminal Justice Reform, 2004).

Office for Public Sector Information, *Forced Marriage (Civil Protection) Act 2007* (The Stationery Office, 2007).

Outsiders, *Disabled People and Paid Sex* (Outsiders, 2006).

Outsiders, *Sex and Learning Disabilities* (Outsiders, 2006).

Plotnikoff J and Woolfson R, *The 'Go-between': Evaluation of Intermediary Pathfinders Projects* (Lexicon Limited, 2005).

Review of Sex and Relationships Education (SRE) in Schools. A Report by the External Steering Group (2008).

Sanders A et al, *Witnesses with Learning Disabilities: Home Office Research Findings – no 44* (Home Office Communications Directorate, 1996).

Sentencing Advisory Panel, *Sentencing Guidelines on Sexual Offences: Consultation Paper* (Sentencing Advisory Panel, 2004).

Sex Education Forum, *Forum Factsheet 32: Sex and Relationships Education for Children and Young People with Learning Disabilities* (Sex Education Forum, 2004).

Social Care Research, *Crime Against People with Learning Disabilities* (Joseph Rowntree Foundation, 1995).

Stevenson K, Davies A and Gunn M, *Blackstone's Guide to the Sexual Offences Act* (Oxford University Press, 2004).

Thompson D and Brown H, *Response-ability: Working with Men with Learning Disabilities who have Abusive or Unacceptable Behaviour* (Mental Health Foundation, 1999).

Thompson D, Clare I C H and Brown H, 'Not such an "ordinary" relationship: the role of women support staff in relation to men with learning disabilities who have difficult sexual behaviour', *Disability and Society*, vol 12, no 4 (1997), 573–592.

UNISON, *The Duty of Care* (UNISON Communications, 2003).

Voice UK, Respond and Mencap, *Behind Closed Doors* (Mencap, 2001).

Voice UK, *Stop! No More Abuse* (Voice UK, 2003).

Wellings K, 'Sexual behaviour in Britain: early heterosexual experience', *Lancet*, vol 358 (2001), 1843–1850.

How fpa can help you

sexual health direct

sexual health direct is a nationwide service run by **fpa**. It provides:

- confidential information and advice and a wide range of booklets on individual methods of contraception, common sexually transmitted infections, pregnancy choices, abortion and planning a pregnancy
- details of contraception, sexual health and genitourinary medicine (GUM) clinics and sexual assault referral centres.

fpa helplines

England
helpline 0845 122 8690
9am to 6pm Monday to Friday

Northern Ireland
helpline 0845 122 8687
9am to 5pm Monday to Thursday
9am to 4.30pm Friday

or visit **fpa**'s website **www.fpa.org.uk**

fpa supporting professionals

fpa *membership*

Become a member of **fpa** and receive a range of benefits while supporting our vital work. The benefits include:

- a full set of **fpa** factsheets and booklets
- quarterly mailings, which include subscriptions to *Sex Talk* and *In Brief*
- discounts on **fpa** open training courses
- discounts on **fpa** publications (school and organisation members).

Choose from three membership packages – individual membership at £30 a year, school membership at £50 a year (includes universities, colleges, Connexions, youth organisations and Sure Start) and organisation membership at £90 a year.

Sex Talk is **fpa**'s newsletter, keeping you in touch with **fpa** events, campaigns and our latest publications and resources. *In Brief* provides the latest news and comment on contraception, sexually transmitted infections and reproductive health.

fpa *training*

fpa provides high quality training in sexual health, sex and relationships, and sexuality. We offer:

- Open training: offered on pre-set dates and open to all.
- On request training: the same content and format as open training but delivered to a specific group or organisation.
- Tailor made training: specifically designed to meet a client's particular needs, and may offer a mix of training and consultation.
- Consultancy: **fpa** has a strong team of experts in all aspects of sexual health who are available to facilitate seminars or briefings, to provide specific advice and to assist with writing a relevant policy or guidelines.

fpa provides university accreditation for some of its courses.

fpa *publications*

fpa offers a complete mail order service for health and education professionals and the public. Our extensive stock includes books, booklets and resources on sex and relationships education, learning disabilities, contraception, and sexual health.

For more details on membership, training or publications see **www.fpa.org.uk** or call 020 7608 5240.